David & Charles Locomotive Studies

THE DRUMMOND GREYHOUNDS OF THE LSWR

D. L. Bradley

DAVID & CHARLES
NEWTON ABBOT LONDON
NORTH POMFRET (VT) VANCOUVER

ISBN 0 7153 7329 3
Library of Congress Catalog Card Number 76-54087

Typeset in 10 on 11 Times New Roman
by HBM Typesetting Limited, Chorley, Lancs
and printed in Great Britain
by Redwood Burn Limited
Trowbridge and Esher
for David & Charles (Publishers) Limited
Brunel House Newton Abbot Devon

Published in the United States of America
by David & Charles Inc
North Pomfret Vermont 05053 USA

Published in Canada
by Douglas David & Charles Limited
1875 Welch Street North Vancouver BC

CONTENTS

PREFACE

This book recounts the long and enthralling history of 66 excellent 4-4-0s which from 1900 until the grouping of railways in 1923 formed the mainstay of London & South Western express services. The brainchild of that eminent and adventurous Scottish locomotive engineer, Dugald Drummond, they were officially classified T9, but on account of their marked propensity for speed, were more generally known as the Greyhounds, a sobriquet they held with honour for no less than 60 years.

Painted an eye-catching apple green, with chocolate, black and white lining, their design was neat and attractive, yet at the same time displaying a quiet air of authority and optimism. In regular service this was fully justified, for they proved the finest express locomotives yet to work on South Western metals. Time and mechanical advancement, however, take but scant account of prowess, no matter how well gained, and by 1922 events had overtaken the class. Fortunately, superheating was to hand and by skilful application a new and invigorated lease of life was injected, which endured throughout Southern Railway days into Nationalisation. At long last the end came in 1961, although one representative evaded the breakers' torches and to-day proudly awaits restoration to working order to take its place among the many other active preserved steam locomotives working on privately-run tourist lines or BR specials.

To set the story of the T9s in perspective the passenger locomotives Drummond designed earlier for the North British and Caledonian Railways cannot be neglected, while coverage is also given to other London & South Western four- and six-coupled express classes – though references to these other classes must be subordinate to the T9s themselves.

This history not only embodies the findings of many years of extensive research into the working of the London & South Western Railway, but also the willing and invaluable help of numerous friends in a diversity of walks of life. In particular, I must mention the assistance and facilities offered by Robert Cogger at the former British Railway Board Museum of Transport at Clapham, the Keeper of the Public Records Office, Porchester Road, London, and the Manager of Eastleigh Locomotive Works. Over several years help and encouragement was also given by E. W. Fry of Salisbury, who not only offered expert advice on the Drummond express classes but found the time to prepare the cylinder drawings and print many of the illustrations. Other aid came from H. C. Casserley, N. Harvey, G. Kerley, S. Nash, R. Roberts and G. Woodward. I am deeply grateful to them all.

Frontispiece: No 773, the Drummond Greyhound built by Dübs & Co for the 1901 Glasgow Exhibition.
[Mitchell Library

Jacket photographs: T9 class 4-4-0 No 708 in July 1899 shortly after delivery by Dübs & Co (front) ; 57 years old and showing no signs of old age No 30285 stands in the evening sunshine in front of Eastleigh Shed in May 1957 (back). *[E W Fry*

CHAPTER ONE

DUGALD DRUMMOND

This celebrated and redoubtable locomotive engineer was born at Ardrossan, Ayrshire, on 1 January 1840 and grew up in the mixed atmosphere of railways and Clyde navigation, for his father was the permanent way inspector of the Bowling Railway. Destined almost from birth to be an engineer, Dugald Drummond served his apprenticeship with Forrest & Barr of Glasgow before gaining greater experience on the Dumbartonshire and Caledonian Railways. Later two years were spent in charge of boiler construction with Thomas Brassey of the Canada Works, Birkenhead, while in mid 1864 he transferred his activities to Cowlairs Locomotive Works of the Edinburgh & Glasgow Railway. There, under the guidance of S. W. Johnson, 16 months were spent as a chargehand in the wheel shop before ambition drove him northwards to Inverness where he became foreman erector of the Highland Railway's Lochgorm Works under William Stroudley.

Thereafter Drummond's rise in railway service was rapid, for in 1867 he was appointed works manager and, when Stroudley departed for the London Brighton & South Coast Railway in February 1870, he was left in charge of the Highland's locomotive affairs until the arrival of David Jones. Later the same year Stroudley found a position for his friend at Brighton, where Drummond remained until promoted Locomotive Superintendent of the North British Railway in February 1875. Seven years later he was again on the move, this time to the neighbouring St Rollox Works of the Caledonian Railway. On this line, as also on the North British, he proved remarkably successful and quickly placed numbers of well-designed goods and passenger locomotives in service. By now approaching middle age and having recently been granted a substantial rise in salary, it might rightly be assumed that he would be content to remain in charge at St Rollox until age forced retirement from the railway scene. This, however, was far from the case, for suddenly in April 1890 he tendered his resignation on deciding with three others to establish the Australasian Locomotive Engine Works in the suburbs of Sydney, New South Wales. This was the consequence of an advertisement in the railway press in May 1889 in which the Commissioner of the New South Wales Railways sought experienced engineers to set up a locomotive repair and construction works within the State on the understanding that orders for the supply of 75 engines and tenders would be placed every five years at prices currently being charged in the United Kingdom and North America.

Unhappily from this point of time Drummond's hitherto excellent fortune deserted him, since within three months insurmountable financial and organisational problems caused abandonment of the scheme. Drummond at once became unemployed and, with no immediate prospects of a return to railway service, he turned in desperation to industrial management and founded the Glasgow Railway Engineering Company. Some success was achieved, but this type of activity had no lasting appeal to a man of Drummond's calibre and, after five years, he gratefully accepted the Locomotive Superintendency of the London & South Western Railway at a salary of £1,500 per annum. Incidentally, this was a much lower remuneration than he had enjoyed on the Caledonian Railway.

Under the benevolent and tactful leadership of William Adams, the works at Nine Elms had been a happy establishment with the minimum of inter-departmental strife or friction. Respect, common sense and mutual trust down to chargehand level was obviously the basis of this enviable state of affairs and one rarely found in large industrial or railway workshops. The Chief at all times fairly exuded friendship and this proved so embracing that all coming in contact gathered the same germ. By this it must not be imagined that Adams was not master of his department, for there was never any doubt of that. Should a gentle hint fail to show a wrongdoer the error of his ways, then a quiet heart to heart talk seldom left the recipient in any doubt as to what would happen if a change of behaviour failed to occur. With Adams' premature retirement because of ill health, Nine Elms Works and the LSWR lost an exceptionally able engineer and a good friend.

As was to be expected, an acceptable replacement proved most difficult to find and quite probably no matter who had been appointed to take charge at Nine Elms he would have been bitterly resented and heartily disliked. Under the circumstances, it would be hard to imagine anyone more likely to fan the flames of dissatisfaction than Dugald Drummond, a dour, explosive and vocal Lowland Scot, devoid of any diplomacy and quite intolerant of the lazy and incompetent. After he took office on 1 August 1895 the Locomotive Department was not left long doubting that it had caught a real tartar, for at once were cast aside all the carefully nurtured principles of friendliness and reticence, and within weeks many long serving and able departmental heads had resigned or accepted early retirement.

Apart from temperament, the main source of friction was the insistence that all departments at Nine Elms should operate independently and have minimal contact, except at the weekly progress meetings held in Drummond's presence. On these occasions, each departmental head gave his report and schedules were agreed for locomotives undergoing or awaiting repair, while attention was given to new construction and the provision of new boilers, fireboxes, cylinders and other major items. Once a repair schedule had been prepared for a locomotive, Drummond insisted that it was adhered to and demanded an explanation if reassembly was delayed by late deliveries to the Erecting Shop. For several months chaos reigned at Nine Elms, but gradually under the able guidance of Robert Urie order was achieved and much to the surprise of many the time spent giving general repairs was reduced by five working days. No longer were men left idle awaiting vital parts while a messenger was hastily despatched to the department in question requesting advice as to its possible time of arrival. Boilers, wheels and other items appeared when required, and work proceeded apace. Success is a great morale booster and by the autumn of 1896, with Nine Elms operating at peak efficiency, the majority of employees drastically reappraised their opinion of Drummond. The new Chief had made his mark and had been accepted.

As time passed, Drummond's bark was found worse than his bite and he let it be known that his staff was expected to speak up and, if in the right, to give as good as they received. Few Southerners could do themselves full justice, but the many Scots who had migrated south with their Chief in 1895 were willing and able to do so. To the discerning, it was abundantly clear that the London & South Western Railway – and the Locomotive Department in particular – had gained the services of a most capable and adventurous engineer. Beneath his dour exterior, Drummond was seen to conceal strong feelings of loyalty and justice, and in later years was spoken of with real affection; his death in November 1912 proved as great a blow as that of his predecessor. He did not always enjoy absolute success, but his aim was extremely high, much higher in fact than most other pre-Grouping locomotive superintendents who tended to perpetuate the known rather than to explore new realms of engineering. Drummond was a man of many roles and of a calibre seldom today found in the highest echelons of industrial management.

Early Drummond 4-4-0 No 479 *Abbotsford,* built for the North British Railway in 1876.

CHAPTER TWO

THE SCOTTISH PRELUDE

There is little doubt that the long and harmonious association with William Stroudley at Cowlairs, Lochgorm and Brighton influenced Dugald Drummond throughout his long and eventful career in railway engineering. At the same time it is equally certain that he gained an altogether wider and grander conception of the steam locomotive's capacity for enlargement and development than ever his mentor was able to create within the confines and special operating pattern of the London Brighton & South Coast Railway.

When taking office at Cowlairs on 1 February 1875 Drummond was the sixth locomotive superintendent of the North British and the one above all others who held the company's destiny firmly clutched in his hands. For, with the impending opening of the new Midland Railway route from Settle to Carlisle and the consequent heavy traffic expected over the North British Waverley line between Carlisle and Edinburgh, new and more powerful locomotives were urgently required. Unfortunately, this line had not been constructed to carry express services for its creation had been piecemeal from a local railway between Edinburgh and Hawick and the Border Union Railway thence to Carlisle. Consequently, the question of curvature, gradients, signalling and station layouts was not granted the same consideration as would have been the case if the future importance of the route had been fully appreciated. Although $98\frac{1}{4}$ miles in length, it was, because of these failings, the most difficult express route in the United Kingdom, especially for heavy, smartly timed trains, and presented Drummond with an unenviable problem, since the company did not possess a single locomotive capable of meeting the performance required.

Brute force alone was no answer, for the locomotives had to be free steaming, smooth riding, at home on the 1 in 70 banks, have good acceleration and daily accept a pounding only the most robust could hope to survive. Aware of this, the railway fraternity – and the Midland in particular – awaited the outcome with great interest. Their attention was aptly rewarded for Drummond designed a class of magnificent 4-4-0s with 6ft 6in coupled wheels, 18in by 24in cylinders, a 4ft 5in diameter boiler and a weight with tender of $76\frac{1}{4}$ tons. The tubes gave a heating surface of 1005sq ft, to which the firebox added a further 94sq ft, making a total of 1099sq ft, while the grate was large with an area of 21sq ft.

There was insufficient time for their construction at Cowlairs, so the work was deputed to Neilson & Co, who offered preferential treatment and early delivery. Even so, they were not available for 1 May 1876, when the Midland commenced running its Scottish Pullman car

North British 4-4-0 No 479 after removal of name and the fitting of lock-up safety valves.

expresses, and one of the earlier North British 4-4-0s had to be equipped with the Westinghouse air brake and specially prepared for the daunting task. Somehow it upheld the honour of the company for 11 days and then rapidly departed from the Waverley route as Nos 476 *Carlisle*, 477 *Edinburgh*, 478 *Melrose* and 479 *Abbotsford* entered traffic.

In service they proved a splendid success and at once removed all Midland qualms of time being lost north of the Border. Four more, Nos 486 *Aberdeen*, 487 *Montrose*, 488 *Galashiels*, and 489 *Hawick*, followed from Neilsons in 1878, while Cowlairs completed Nos 490 *St Boswells*, 491 *Dalhousie*, 492 *Newcastleton*, and 493 *Netherby*. They were well liked by the men and Drummond himself was so well pleased with their performance that he used the design as a pattern for all his later 4-4-0s until the South Western D15s of 1912. What then was the basis of their success? No single factor was accountable, although to the fore was the boiler with its excellent proportions, deep firebox, large grate, 150lb working pressure and prodigious capacity for steam. To this essential constituent Drummond added a well-designed front end which permitted a fair degree of expansive working and exhibited as great an advance on current thinking as did the Churchward 4-6-0s of the 20th century. The direct Stephenson valve gear with trough slide bars was robustly constructed and operated valves with divided ports, while the exhaust steam was discharged via passages cast round the exterior of the cylinders. The last-

Left: At first glance North British 4-4-0 No 486 could easily be mistaken for a London & South Western Greyhound.

Bottom left: A change of railway, but all the Drummond characteristics remain: Caledonian Railway 4-4-0 No 79 *Carbrook* of 1889.

Below: Drummond's final design for the Caledonian Railway, No 91 of 1891.

mentioned flanked the steam chests and with 27in centres offered ample space between the cranks for four eccentrics without the necessity of skimping webs or dishing wheels. The main bearings were likewise well proportioned, which encouraged good mileages between repairs and gave the ability to withstand the hard pounding demanded by the tortuous Waverley line. The general appearance was attractive and workmanlike with many features which over the next 25 years became the hallmark of Dugald Drummond practice.

Other equally successful and well-designed classes were introduced over the next few years before Drummond resigned from the company's service in August 1882 to become Locomotive Superintendent of the neighbouring Caledonian Railway at a salary of £1,700 per annum. Despite his achievements at Cowlairs, Drummond's seven years with the North British were not particularly congenial or tranquil for after the jovial Tom Wheatley the men found him abrupt and uncommunicative, and from time to time crises arose which could only be resolved by intervention of the directors. On one memorable occasion the erecting shop work force walked out on strike following the dismissal of a foreman found smoking on duty, while in April 1881 many crews refused to take their engines off the running sheds when the driver of a goods train was disciplined for a minor pitch-in caused by a signalling error. Probably all concerned were well satisfied by the transfer of allegiance.

At St Rollox Drummond became the custodian of a sound if antiquated stock of locomotives, almost all of which had outside cylinders. Singles worked all the best express services, except those between Edinburgh and Glasgow, Perth and Aberdeen, and Dundee, Perth and Glasgow, where 2-4-0s of various vintages had charge. Only five 4-4-0s were available, built by Neilson & Co in 1877 to the order of Ben Conner, and not of a particularly successful design. Unusually for the period and for a line having such extensive and profitable goods and mineral traffic, almost all locomotives were of the four-coupled type.

Once again, there was an urgent call for new and more powerful express locomotives, and while the plans were being prepared Drummond rebuilt a number of Conner goods 2-4-0s into respectable stop-gap passenger locomotives by the simple expedient of fitting free steaming boilers and adjusting the balancing. Altogether four new classes were introduced: 6ft 6in 4-4-0 express passenger, 0-6-0 (the Jumbos) goods, 5ft 9in 4-4-0 (Coast Bogies) passenger and 0-4-4 suburban tanks. The last two classes were

relatively small and intended for local duties and, though good in themselves, were quickly replaced by more powerful types. Of the Jumbo goods, it is sufficient to relate that they proved so generally useful and capable that many remained active until long after nationalisation in 1948.

The 28 6ft 6in 4-4-0s entered traffic over a period of seven years, the first ten from Neilson & Co in 1884 and the remainder in batches from St Rollox between 1885 and 1891. In relation to the work expectation of the Caledonian's Glasgow–Carlisle main line, the boiler heating surface was not over-generous, although close attention to the cylinder steam utilisation ensured that this proved no major handicap. The 16 1884/85 engines closely followed the North British series, but instead of the slide bars being attached to the cylinder block they were secured at mid length by the motion plate to give support where stresses were liable to be greatest. The absence of any obstruction to the rear of the bars permitted the expansion link being positioned further forward than otherwise would have been possible, which in turn lengthened the eccentric rods and reduced the lead increase when engines were notched up. It was an important concession on a line having the characteristics and heavy loadings of that between Glasgow and Carlisle.

With these excellent 4-4-0s in traffic there was no need for more express locomotives for some years, and Drummond was able to devote time and resources to satisfying other needs. However, in 1886 two express locomotives of obvious Caledonian lineage were displayed at the Edinburgh Exhibition, No 123, a 4-2-2-built by Neilson & Co, and No 124, a 4-4-0 built by Dübs & Co. At the close of the exhibition both entered Caledonian service. Today it is difficult to suggest whether the railway company or these two firms proposed their construction, although it is quite certain that both had Drummond's active co-operation. To a large extent the single, No 123, was based on the 1884/85 66 class 4-4-0s, but its slide bars were attached to the cylinders and the motion plate while the slightly smaller boiler was pitched higher in the frames. Other modifications included compressed air sanding, steel frames and an Adams-type vortex blast pipe.

No 124, the Dübs 4-4-0, also followed the 66 class, although its front end was completely remodelled to take Bryce-Douglas valve gear, larger cylinders, improved lubrication and vertical screw reverser akin to that employed by Drummond on his North British locomotives. The valve gear had some affinity with the Joy system for there was a link attached to the connecting rod, while, because of some of the valve spindle's movement being derived from the crosshead, some similarity could also be claimed with the Walschaerts gear. It had been employed with some success in marine engines where better steam distribution gave a fuel saving of 7 per cent, but in railway service the large number of pins caused excessive wear and regular failures.

Although both engines remained solitary members of their respective classes, they did influence future Caledonian construction commencing with the small-wheeled Coast Bogies of 1888. Features perpetuated from No 123 included the vortex blast pipe, steel frames and compressed air sanding, while use was made of the layout at the rear of No 124.

During 1888 a paper on compound locomotives presented to the Institute of Civil Engineers evoked much interest and discussion, and led Drummond to approach his directors for authority to build a compound goods or passenger locomotive in order to test the relative merits of otherwise similar machines. Permission was refused, so Drummond decided to explore the possibility of gaining the economy claimed for compounding by using simple locomotives employing higher than standard working pressures. Fortunately, this decision coincided with the necessity of providing more express locomotives for the Carlisle–Perth service and for the through engine workings between Carlisle and Aberdeen introduced the previous year. Consequently, six new 4-4-0s were ordered from St Rollox in December 1888 and delivered at a cost of £2,110 each late the following year. Although outwardly similar to the 1884/85 series, they embodied a number of innovations which placed them even further ahead of current practice, the most important being at the front end. There, to gain short and direct passages, the steam ports were repositioned at the ends of the valve face, while the slide valves were divided and each provided with a separate exhaust port. As in the 66 class, all ports were divided horizontally into equal upper and lower portions with steam from the lower halves of the exhaust ports gaining the blast pipe by passages circumventing the outside of the cylinders. A difference was the use of the main framing to form the outer walls of these passages. Other

Above: The Edinburgh International Exhibition 4-2-2 No 123.

changes included vertical screw reversing, longer eccentric rods, and steel boilers and frames.

The result was a remarkable class of free-running and economical 4-4-0s with the capability of high power output relative to the cylinder and boiler dimensions. In 1889, a series of trials were run between Edinburgh and Carlisle with engines working at pressures of 150, 175 and 200lb/sq in so that Drummond could test the validity of his contention that well-designed simple locomotives with high working pressure could give comparable economies to compounds. In this, the tests proved him correct, but his success was short lived, for when left to their own devices drivers refused to employ expansive working and thereby dissipated much of the gains offered. Consequently, all engines reverted to 150lb pressure and when further 4-4-0s were required in 1890 a return was made to the front end layout of the 1884/85 66 class. These later 4-4-0s entered traffic after Drummond left St Rollox and, together with six more of generally similar design built in 1894 by his successor, John Lambie, made sure that no break in tradition occurred before John F. McIntosh became the Caledonian's locomotive superintendent in 1895.

The 20 years from 1875 to 1895 had seen little change in the size of boiler fitted to British locomotives, but the gradual introduction of heavier permanent way, improved drainage and strength-

Below: Fig 1 Arrangement of cylinders and valves on Caledonian 66 class 4-4-0s, 1884–6 series.

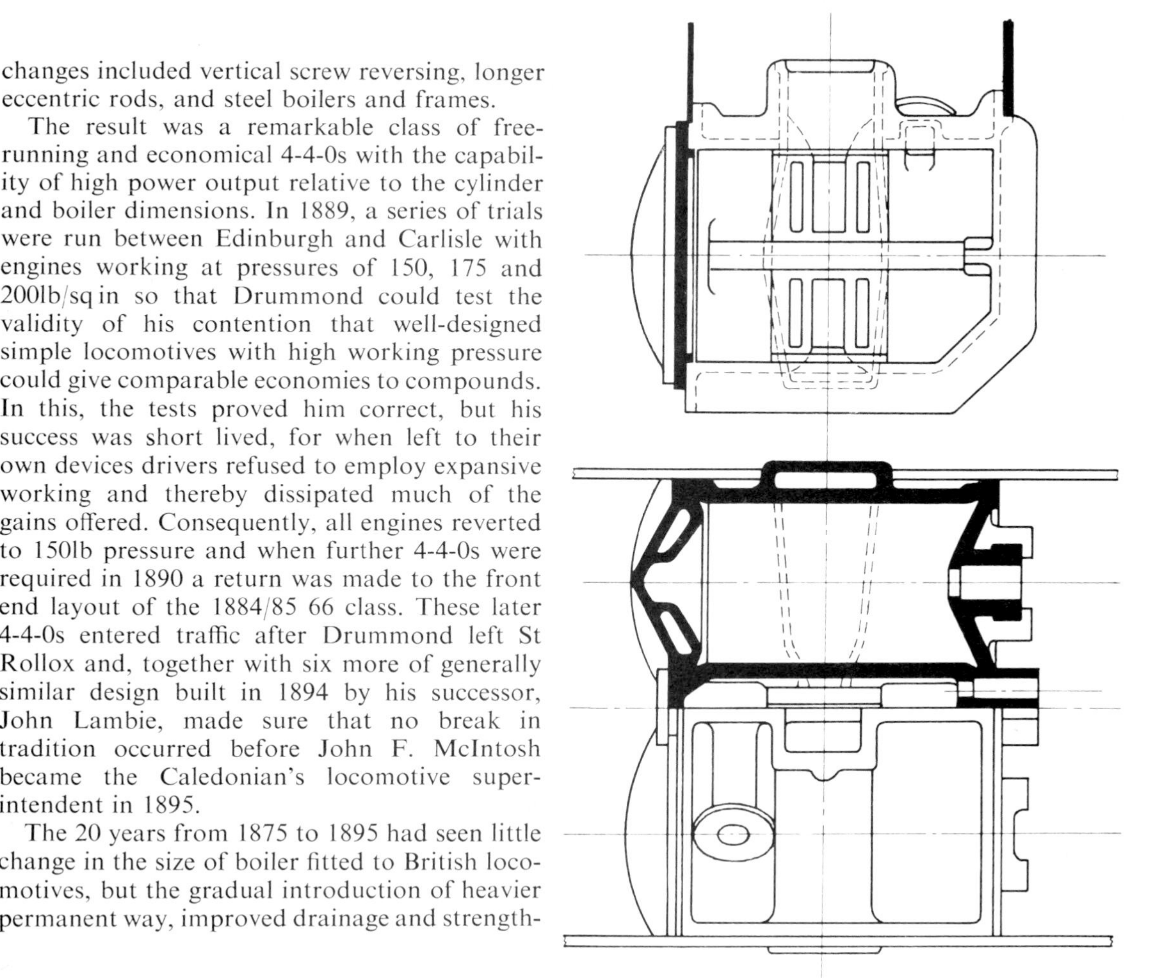

Above: Caledonian 4-2-2 No 123 at speed near Aberdeen, August 1891.

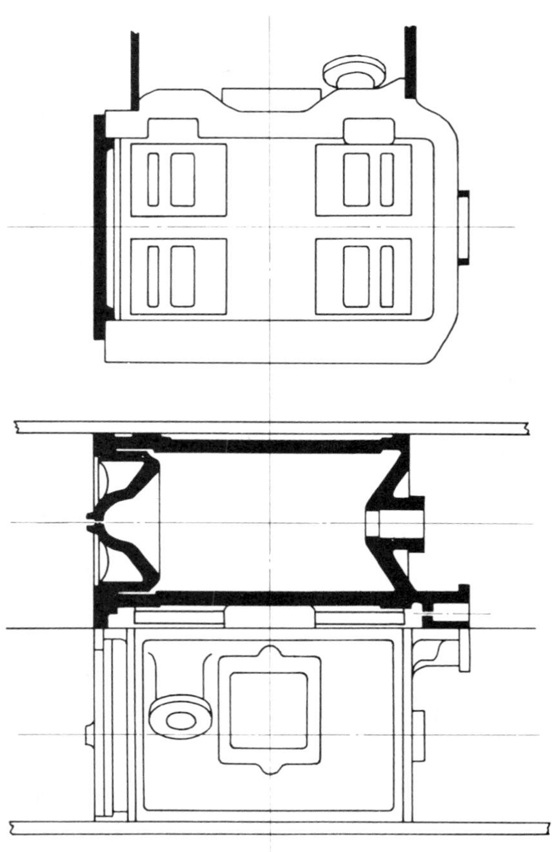

Left: Fig 2 Arrangement of cylinders and valves on Caledonian 1883 series engines of class 66, Nos 76–9, 84 and 87.

ened bridges now made possible radical increases in boiler size and weight. Of this McIntosh was truly appreciative and took full advantage of the possibilities offered in designing and building his Dunalastair I 4-4-0s of 1896 for, apart from the enlarged boiler and grate, they were a precise development of the Drummond–Lambie series. In service their feats of haulage and speed became legend, not only in Scotland but throughout the British Isles. Their outstanding merit lay in an almost unlimited capacity for steam generation, although of almost equal importance was the ability to employ it efficiently whether driven expansively or by use of the regulator and longer cut-offs. Later enlarged and improved versions of the class entered traffic until the Caledonian Railway possessed the best series of express 4-4-0s to be found on any pre-grouping line. Much of this success can be traced to Dugald Drummond.

CHAPTER THREE

NINE ELMS – 1895 TO 1901

On taking office at Nine Elms on 1 August 1895, Drummond had the good fortune to find the London & South Western Railway's locomotive affairs in such excellent order that he was able to assess methodically the line's motive power requirements before committing himself to positive action. This was the consequence of the foresight and engineering skill of William Adams who had been in charge of Nine Elms Works between 1878 and 1895. During this period he had introduced a succession of handsome and capable outside cylinder 4-4-0s with both 6ft 7in and 7ft 1in coupled wheels, each being a progressive improvement and enlargement of its predecessor. A number remained on order at his retirement and these Drummond was pleased to complete, with but minor modifications. Of the older passenger locomotives, only a handful of Beattie 2-4-0s and 4-4-0s remained active on local duties, all being scheduled for early replacement.

Drummond, during his prolonged and unsought rustication from the locomotive world of the major railway companies, was only able to observe from afar the many changes and improvements of these eventful years. Nevertheless, he maintained a vigorous interest in the various happenings, none more so than those of the Midland Railway where the acceptance of higher axle loadings and the introduction of steam sanding had led to a revival of singles for main line express work. Drummond was greatly impressed by their speed, free running and economic working, although at the same time considering that the loads and gradients of the Bournemouth line called for more adhesion than was possible with a single set of driving wheels. This apprehension was overcome in a 'double-single' design, in which two inside cylinders drove the leading driving wheels and the outside pair the trailing drivers. With the absence of coupling rods, the wheel arrangement became 4-2-2-0. The drawings were presented by Drummond to the Locomotive Committee on 6 January 1897, when the construction of one engine was authorised at a cost of £2,815, including the tender. Numbered 720, this interesting locomotive was completed by Nine Elms Works in August 1897 when, after a brief running-in period, it was set to work on the

LSWR T7 class 4-2-2-0 double-single No 720, Dugald Drummond's first express locomotive for the London & South Western Railway.

Above: E10 class 4-2-2-0 double-single No 372 at the head of a West of England express, June 1917.
[H. Gordon Tidey

Below: The Drummond double bogie 4000 gallon tender, and E10 class No 373 in March 1910.

Bournemouth expresses. Unfortunately it was with limited success, for drivers found it virtually impossible to start heavy trains, while the boiler proved quite incapable of supplying the volume of steam necessary to satisfy the voracious demands of the four 15in cylinders. Such was the clamour of dissatisfaction raised by the various drivers' lobbies that Drummond, on 29 September 1897, took the unprecedented step of meeting a deputation of senior drivers at Waterloo to explain his choice of design. The men listened, but were not entirely convinced and in the following month requested a further audience when their fears were only mollified by the information that 10 conventional four-coupled express locomotives were to be built in 1898. Drummond did not, however, promise to withdraw No 720 from traffic and, with typical Scottish tenacity, at once attempted to make it more acceptable for express service by the use of smaller cylinders and later by the fitting of a much larger boiler. At the same time five more generally similar double-singles, Nos 369–73 were constructed at Nine Elms. Once experience of their eccentricities had been gained, all gave reasonably useful service with lightly loaded expresses, although seldom was their performance comparable with that of similarly dimen-

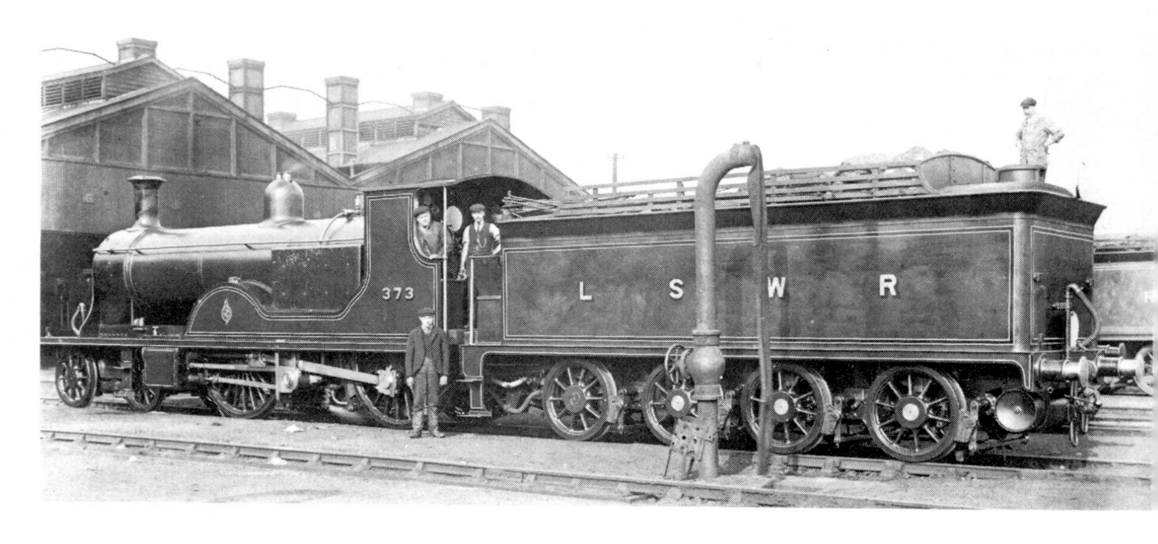

sioned 4-4-0s and because of this all six double-singles had a much shorter life.

Drummond's persistence with expensive locomotives of a type whose usefulness in general service was so obviously questionable has frequently given rise to comment, although no-one has offered a satisfactory answer. A detailed study of the current railway scene suggests that Drummond remained intrigued with the economies credited to compounding and yet had come to believe that entirely adequate compound locomotives could not be constructed within the confines of the British loading gauge. He also questioned whether drivers could be trained to operate them to full advantage; thus he looked elsewhere and found the Midland singles as a possible alternative by which similar operational savings could be gained without the complications of compounding. In his double-singles he attempted to retain the unfettered running of the Midland engines, yet at the same time to gain much of the adhesion of the 4-4-0s. He failed, but credit must be given to his courage and foresight at a period in our locomotive history when few engineers expressed interest in more economic working of their motive power.

The 10 4-4-0s referred to by Drummond in September 1897 were ordered from Nine Elms at an estimated cost of £1,875 each on 19 January 1898. Apparently some misjudgment occurred with this approximation of building costs, for when despatched to traffic as Nos 290 to 299 between June and November 1898, they were booked out at £2,295. Dimensions were:

Cylinders	$18\frac{1}{2}$in × 26in
Bogie	3ft 7in
Coupled wheels	6ft 7in
Wheelbase	6ft 6in + 6ft 9in + 9ft = 22ft 3in
Boiler diameter	4ft 5in
Boiler length	10ft 6in
Firebox length	6ft 4in
Heating surfaces:	
Tubes	1,068sq ft
Firebox	124sq ft
Total	1,192sq ft
Grate area	$20\frac{1}{2}$sq ft
Working pressure	175lb
Weight in working order:	
Bogie	15tons 13cwt
Leading coupled wheels	17tons 6cwt
Trailing coupled wheels	13tons 17cwt
Total	46tons 16cwt
Tender	40tons 14cwt
Engine and tender	87tons 10cwt

Known as the C8 class, they were similar in design and appearance to engines built earlier by Drummond for the North British and Caledonian Railways. The boiler was of steel in two rings with the dome mounted on the rearmost and capped by a pair of lock-up safety valves in neat brass covers. Wingplates completed the smokebox, and sandboxes were incorporated in the leading splashers, while the cab contours followed those of the Caledonian 4-4-0s.

Drummond's first London & South Western 4-4-0, C8 class No 290 at Nine Elms, June 1908.

The direct Stephenson link motion was of robust construction with the motion plate positioned midway along the slide bars where maximum stress occurred. Further advantages came from the 12in longer than standard eccentric rods, which gave improved lead events, and from the generous bearing surfaces of the valve spindle bushes housed in the motion plate. To avoid the undesirable conduction of heat from the cylinders to the slipper blocks, the slide bars were not connected to the cylinder casting at the leading end, while equally practical was their trough pattern which partially enclosed the crossheads and protected the working surfaces from ash, sand and other abrasive substances never long absent from steam locomotives. The pistons were conical in order to accommodate

Right: A C8 class boiler under construction in Nine Elms Works, April 1898.

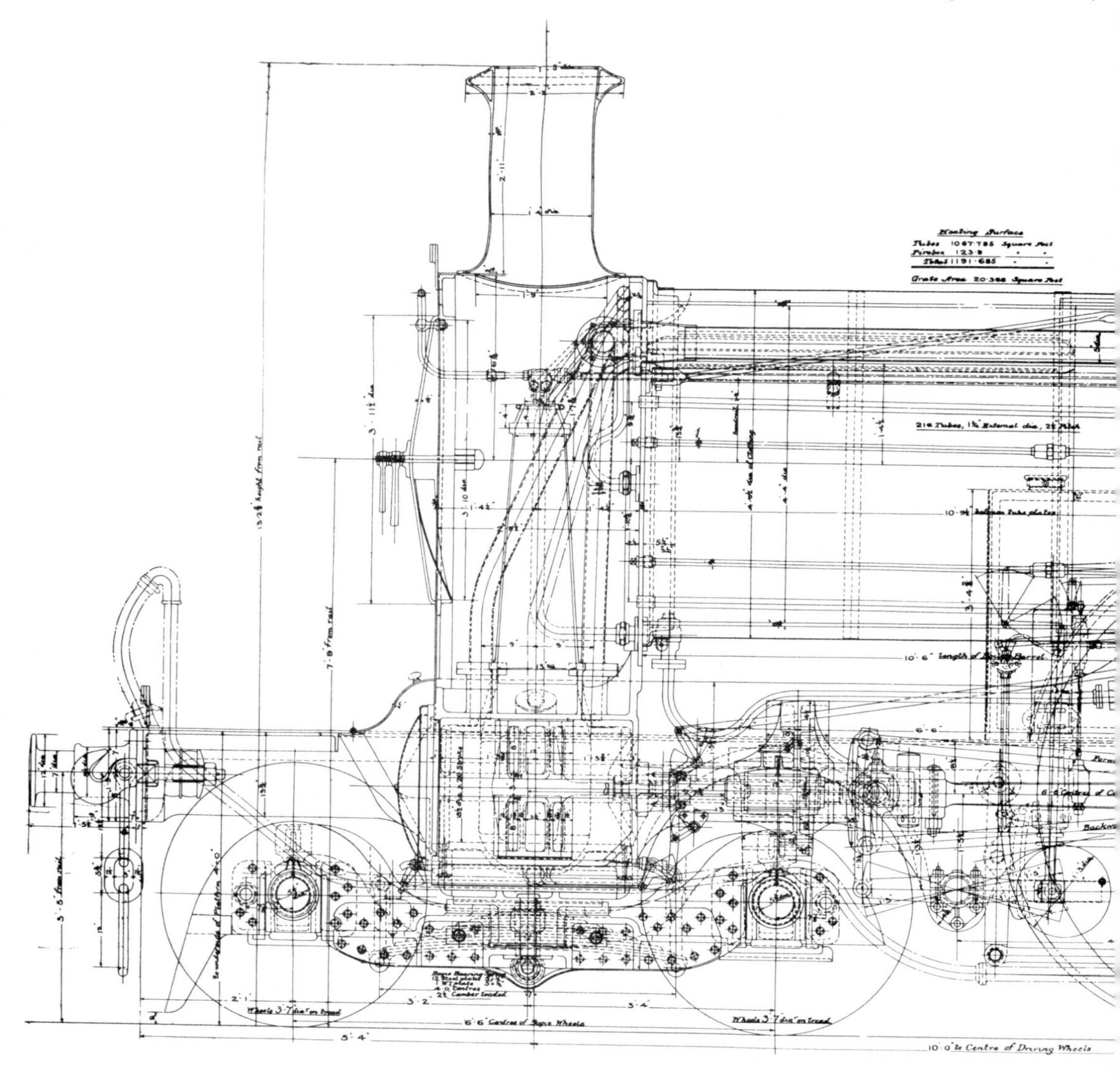

Below: Fig 3 General arrangement drawing of Drummond LSW C8 class 4-4-0. *[British Railways*

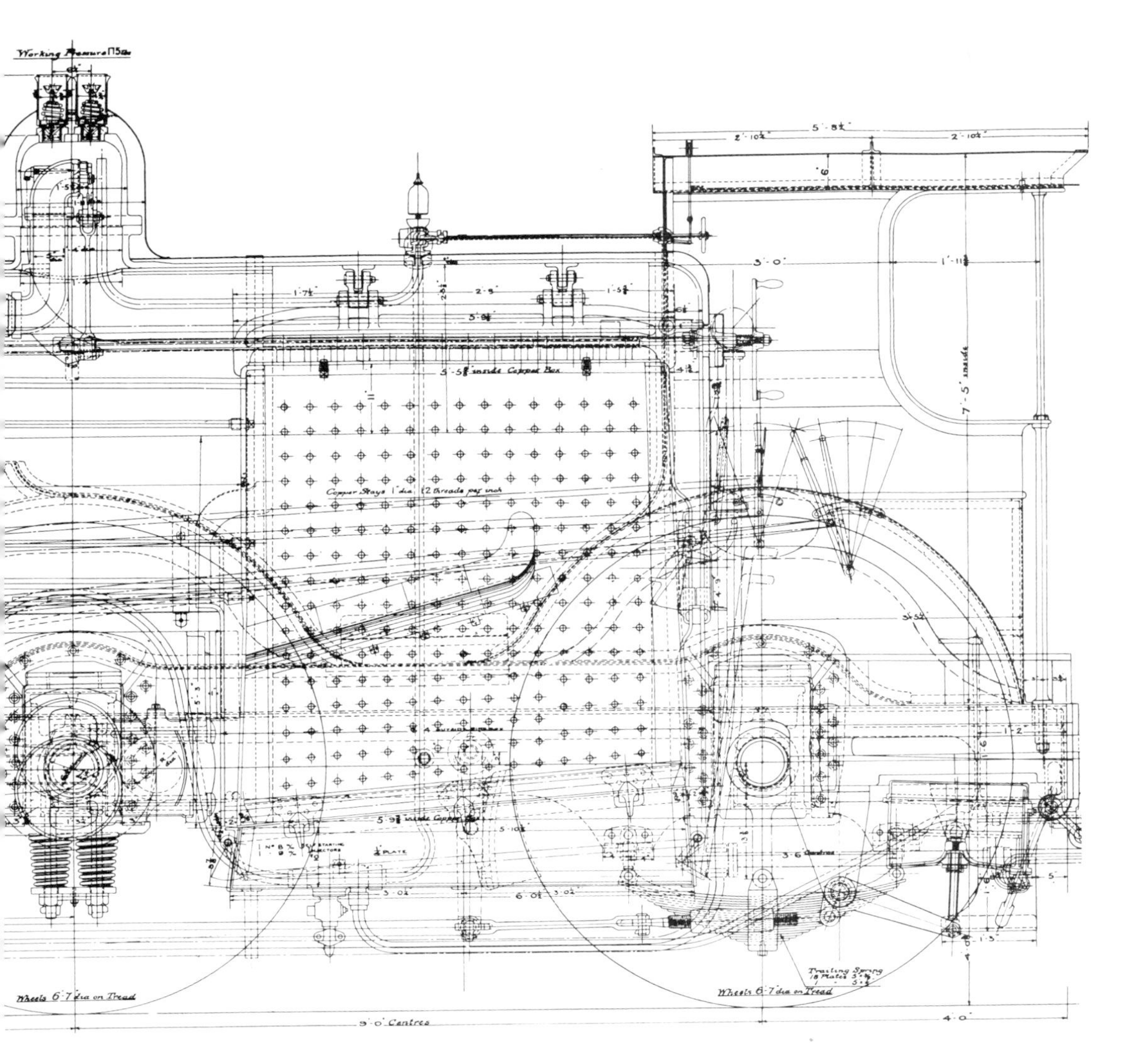

Copper Stays 1" dia. 12 threads per inch
7'-5" inside
Wheels 6'-7 dia on Tread
Wheels 6'-7 dia on Tread
9'-0" Centres

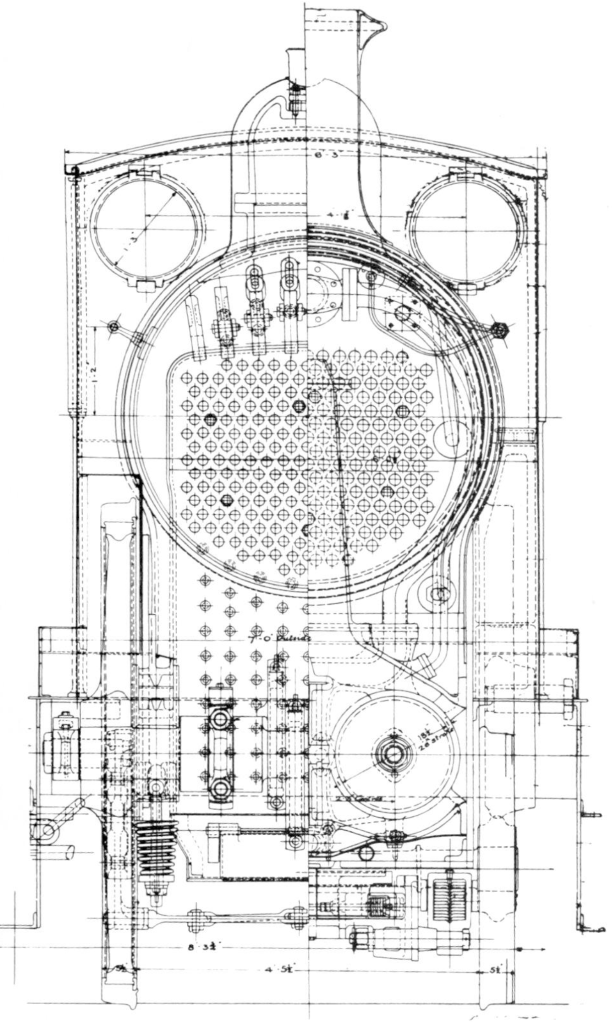

longer connecting rods, these being of rectangular section with marine type big ends.

Set at 2ft 3in centres, the cylinders were bored out to a diameter of 18½in with 1in thick barrels. The steam chests were sited between the cylinders, but, despite this, were unusually spacious with the exhaust ports divided into separate halves, one above and the other below the horizontal centre line. The exhaust steam passages from the lower set passed round the cylinders, widening as they progressed until at the sides, where the frames formed the retaining walls, they were almost as wide as the cylinders were long. This presented a cross-sectional area of ample dimensions for half the steam from one cylinder.

The six-wheeled tender carried four tons of coal and 3,500 gallons of water, and apart from coal rails was reminiscent of those provided in earlier years for the Scottish engines. The 14ft wheelbase was equally divided, while the boxes were outside and the springs overhung where both could be readily inspected and maintained. The overall length and capacity was the same as tenders provided for the 1897 Dübs-built 700 class six-coupled goods, but the wheelbase was 1ft greater.

In traffic the engines proved trouble-free and most durable, although quickly gaining the reputation of hunting badly at speed, especially when engines were running down banks with steam off. All went new to Nine Elms shed and at once were rostered for the Bournemouth and Salisbury expresses in place of the Adams 4-4-0s. On the former they gave a reasonably good account of themselves, but the heavier and more smartly timed West of England services showed

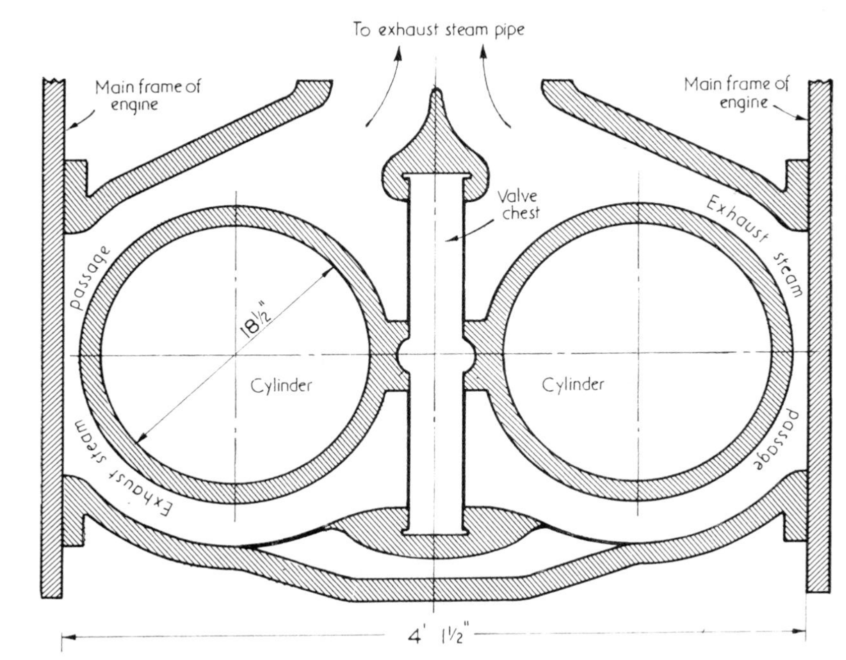

Left: C8 class No 293 at Strawberry Hill in July 1921, with 4000 gallon tender, transfer numerals and Urie power classification.
[Locomotive Publishing Co

Below left: Fig 4 Cross section of C8 class.

Right: Fig 5 Standard Drummond LSWR arrangement for 18½ × 26in cylinders.

Below: Fig 6 Drummond 3500 gallon tender.
[British Railways

the boiler's deficiency. It was similar to those fitted to the 700 and M7 classes and was probably employed in the interests of standardisation, but like other eminent locomotive engineers Drummond discovered that the steam demands of goods engines and suburban tanks were less exacting than those of express locomotives. Standardisation offered many advantages, but it was also open to pitfalls. As a result all 10 C8s were quietly removed from the heaviest express duties and relegated to the Waterloo–Portsmouth and Salisbury–Exeter semi-fasts. They were also used on excursions and specials where loads were moderate and speed unimportant.

Apparently, the possibility of this boiler deficiency had not escaped Drummond, for on 2 February 1898, some months before the first C8 entered traffic, he invited tenders for the construction of 30 larger 4-4-0s, the T9s. Altogether seven manufacturers responded and the replies were read over by the Locomotive Committee on 16 March 1898, when the lowest of £2,945 by Dübs & Co was found acceptable. Details of the other offers were: Neilson & Co £3,117; Sharp, Stewart & Co £3,150; Vulcan Foundry £3,190; Beyer Peacock & Co £3,220; Kitson & Co £3,360; and Robert Stephenson & Co £3,800. Considering the cheapness of the Dübs offer,

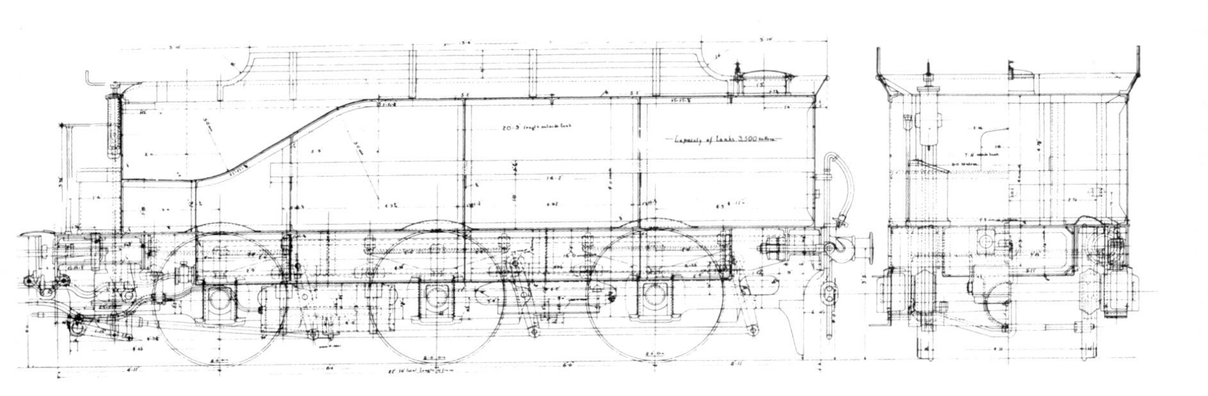

Above: The Drummond cross-firebox watertubes of No 702 with the inspection covers open.

Right: Fig 7 Dimensions of T9 class crank axle.

Below: No 705 at Nine Elms in April 1900 with 3500 gallon tender, number plates and firebox watertubes. One of the clackboxes is just visible on the front tube-plate behind the smokebox saddle.

one wonders if they anticipated a profit or whether the order was so urgently required to keep the work force employed that they were prepared to accept bare costs or possibly a small loss.

The original drawings indicated the fitting of conventional fireboxes, but on 30 March 1898, Drummond wrote intimating a wish to modify the design to incorporate cross water tubes. Dübs agreed to the modifications provided the price per engine and tender was increased by £255 to £3,200. At a later date minor changes were made to the smokebox layout, the bogie springing and injector positioning, but they were found acceptable without any further addition to the price.

In appearance they were very similar to the earlier class, although readily identifiable by the firebox cross water tubes. These were in two nests, one consisting of 36 and the other 25 tubes, 2½in in diameter and 3ft 7in long which lay across the firebox above the centre line with prominent external rectangular covers for inspection and maintenance. The 1in thick steel plate frames were 29ft 4in in length and were particularly strongly braced, which enabled the class to withstand the ravages of time and hard work extremely well, for few cracks were noticeable in the framing 50 years later. Generous bearings gave a notable freedom from hot boxes and ensured that good mileages were run between repairs.

The boiler, apart from the firebox, was

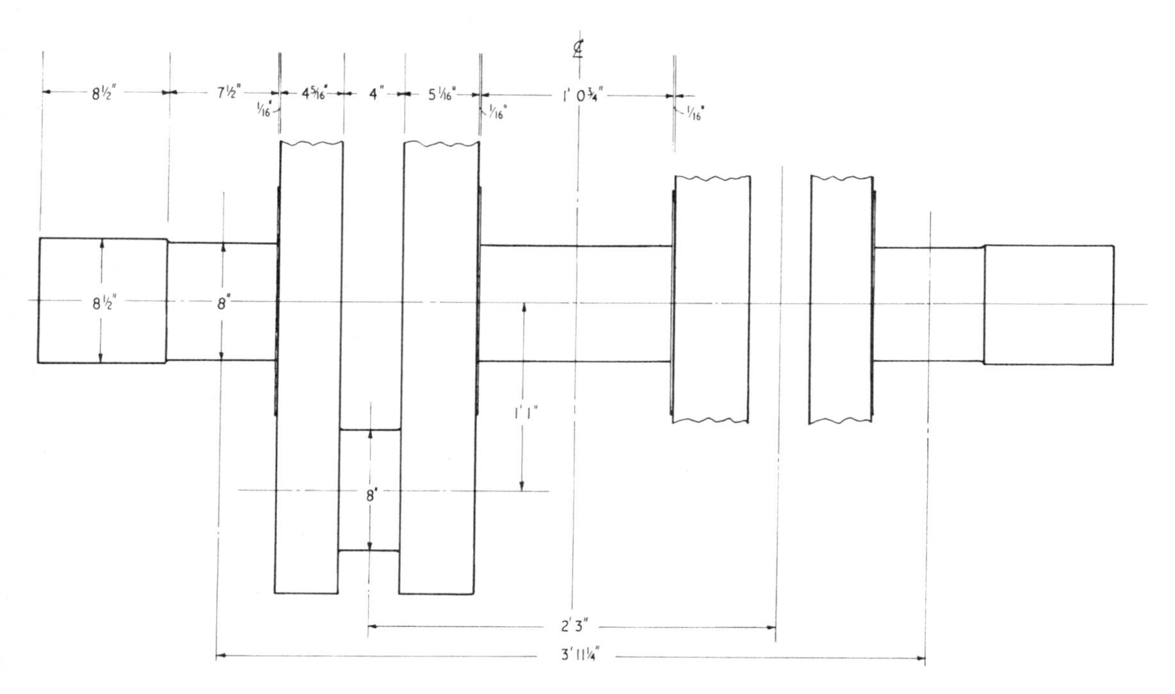

basically similar to that carried by the C8s, and incidentally also that fitted to the Drummond 700 goods and the M7 0-4-4 tanks. The clack boxes were positioned beneath the barrel, immediately to the rear of the smokebox, with the feed water being conveyed through the smokebox by coiled copper pipes so that as much heat as possible was absorbed before finally entering the boiler at the centre of the tubeplate. The chimney was of the well-proportioned lipped pattern employed successfully with but minor differences on all the Drummond 4-4-0s until the large-boilered S11s and L12s of 1903/05. It was also used on the Adams classes as and when renewal of their stove pipes became necessary, although on this engineer's 4-4-0s the application was neither an aesthetic nor a practicable success for there was little harmony with the boiler mountings and moreover, some loss of steam capacity. Drummond, throughout his career in railway service, had a violent dislike of stove pipe chimneys. Therefore, it is strange to relate that on becoming locomotive superintendent in turn of the North British, Caledonian and London & South Western Railways he found this type of chimney in general use, for it had been favoured by Wheatley and Conner, as well as Adams. By the time Nine Elms was reached, he must have begun to wonder whether fate was tilted against him.

Delivery was promised before 31 December 1899, but a strike in the boiler shop at Dübs delayed the assembly of the last five for several weeks. Nos 702–19 and 721–27 reached Nine Elms between February and October 1899, with Nos 728–32 following at the end of January 1900, the works numbers being 3746–75. In appearance they were generally similar to the C8s, but the coupled wheelbase was lengthened to 10ft to accommodate the longer firebox. Changed details were:

Wheelbase	6ft 6in + 6ft 9in + 10ft = 23ft 3in
Firebox length	7ft 4in
Grate area	24sq ft
Heating surfaces:	
Tubes (280 × 1½in)	1,186½sq ft
Firebox	148¼sq ft
Firebox water tubes	165 sq ft
Total	1,499¾sq ft
Weight in working order:	
Bogie	15tons 0cwt
Leading coupled wheels	17tons 12cwt
Trailing coupled wheels	15tons 10cwt
Total	48tons 2cwt

The cab and splashers of these T9s were not extended to the platform edge, and this necessitated the provision of separate casings to accommodate the coupling rods. At the time these rods were exceptionally long and Drummond took special care with their design and construction to make sure they could accept the stresses and strains of main line service. Once

L S W R

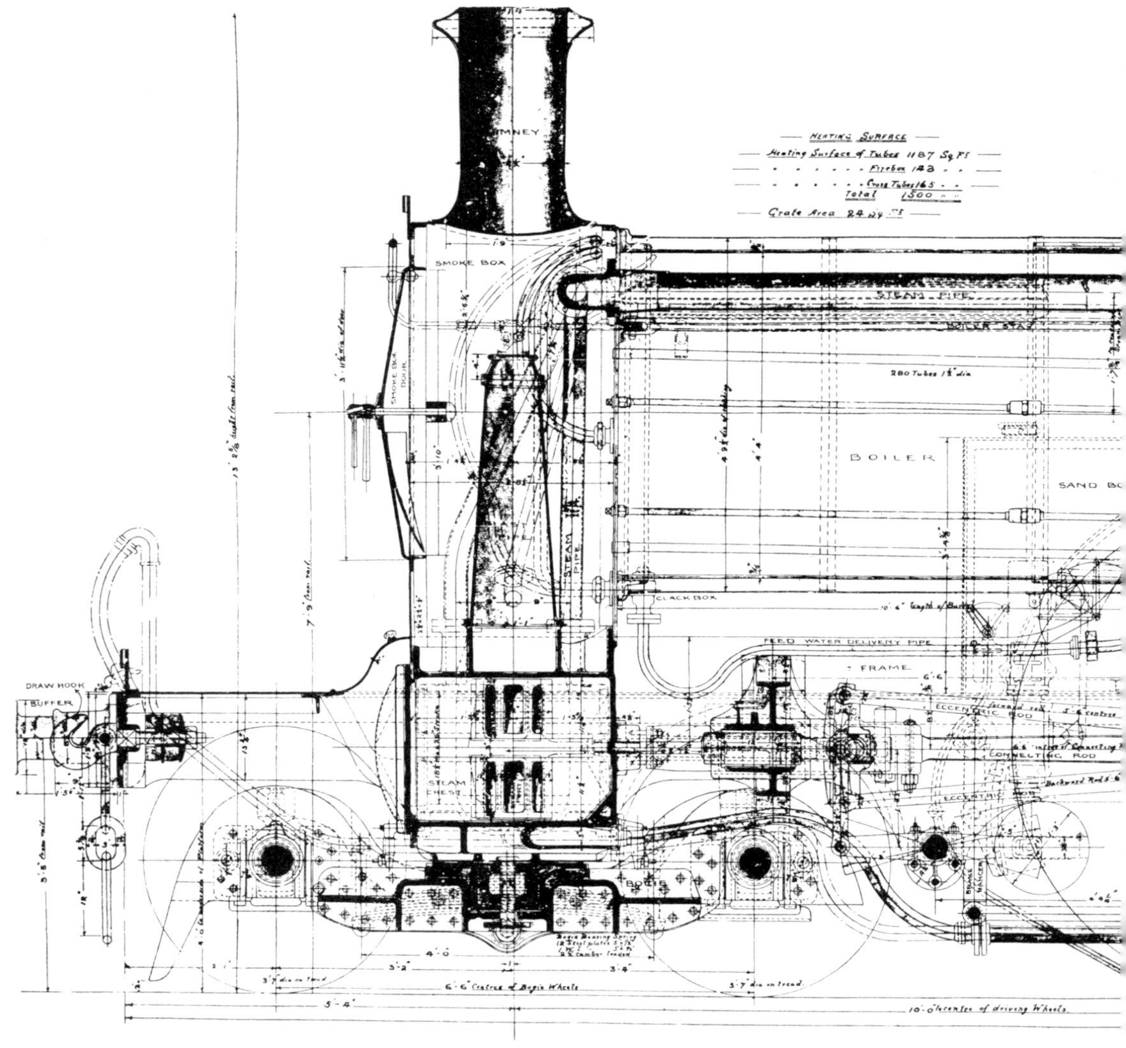
HEATING SURFACE
Heating Surface of Tubes 1187 Sq Ft
Firebox 148
Cross Tubes 165
Total 1500
Grate Area 24 sq ft
SMOKE BOX
STEAM PIPE
BOILER STAY
BOILER
CLACK BOX
FEED WATER DELIVERY PIPE
FRAME
DRAW HOOK
BUFFER
STEAM CHEST
CONNECTING ROD
6'-6" Centres of Bogie Wheels
10'-0" centres of driving Wheels

Left: No 287 in February 1903, one of the 1899–1900 series with conventional fireboxes.

Below: Fig 8 General arrangement drawing of Drummond T9 class 4-4-0 of the Dübs series built in 1899. [*British Railways*

again, the large sandboxes were combined with the leading splashers and, by gravity, fed sand ahead of the driving wheels. No provision was made for the trailing coupled wheels, but for tender-first working a small container was available on the right side of the tender with a pipe directing sand to the rail tops. This unfortunately was so far from the coupled wheels that the practical value was minimal for much was swept away by wind or rain before performing a useful service! Left-hand drive was fitted, the regulator being of the Stroudley double handle pattern, while reversing was by steam. The latter proved expensive to maintain, but otherwise gave excellent service and was not plagued by slip on the road like so many other steam reversers. Altogether the design of these engines was neat,

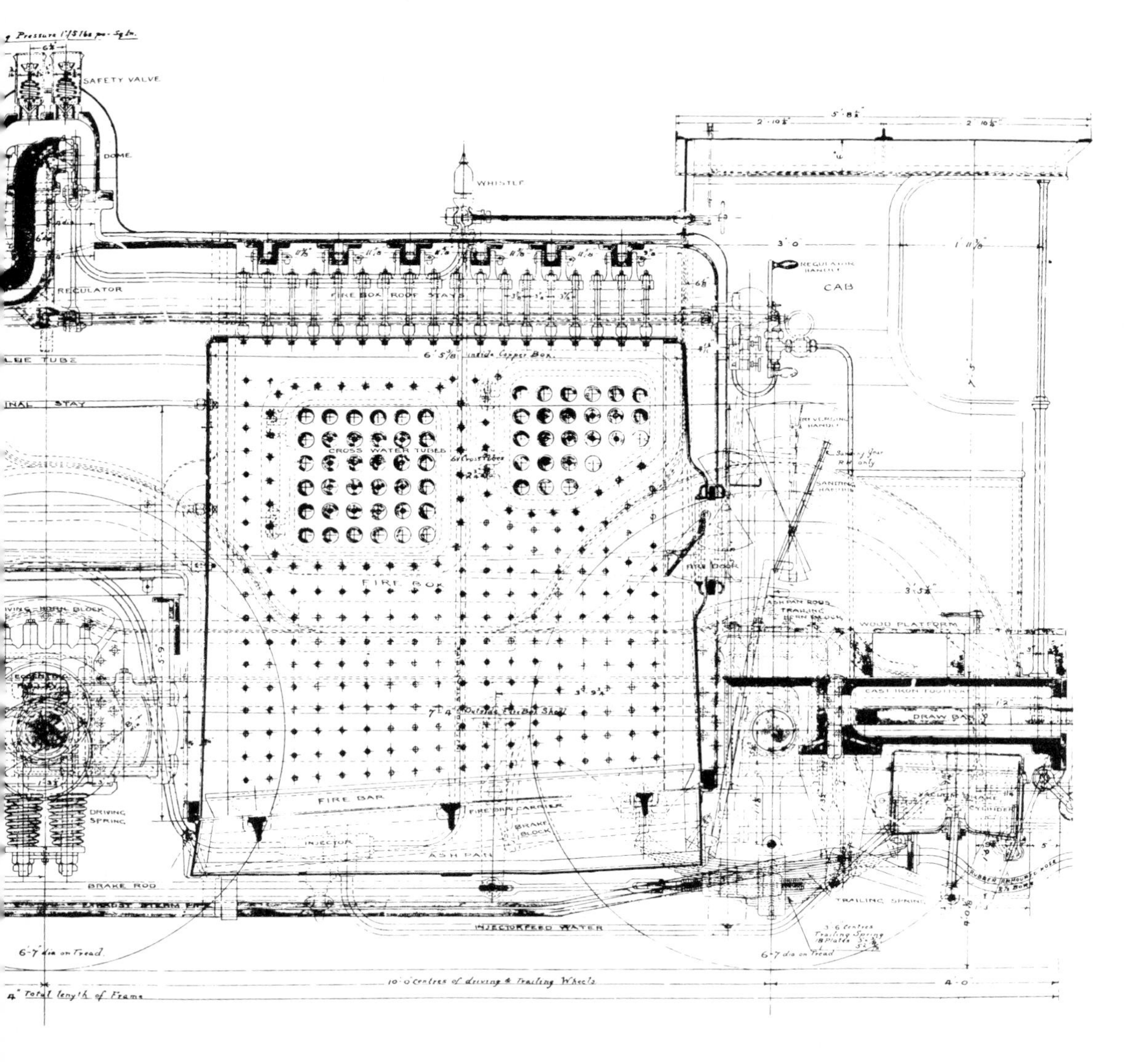

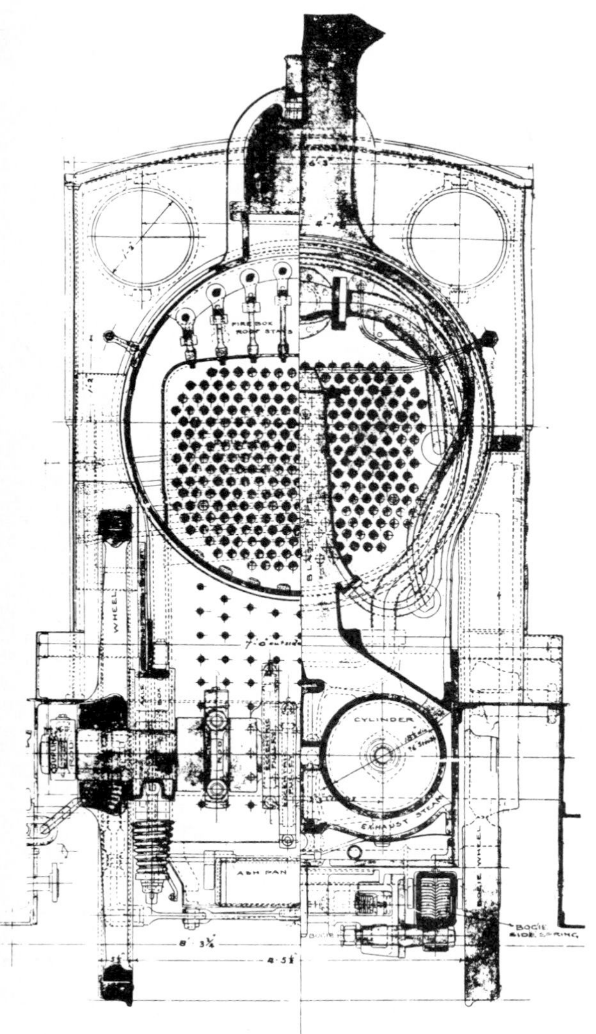

Left: Fig 9 Cross section of Dübs 1899 series T9. *[British Railways*

Right: Final series Greyhound No 312 in May 1901, with wide cab, full width splashers, numberplates, firebox watertubes, 4000 gallon tender and smokebox sand containers.

Below right: Fig 10 Drummond 4000 gallon double bogie tender. *[British Railways*

simple and attractive, and a credit to Dugald Drummond.

A further engine, No 773, was constructed by Dübs & Co for display at the 1901 Glasgow Exhibition and after closure was delivered to the LSWR on 12 December 1901. Dübs wrote to the company on 28 February 1900 requesting permission to exhibit a Drummond 4-4-0 and at the same time offering its sale at £3,525. The directors readily authorised the construction and display, but refused acceptance until the price was reduced to £3,200, including delivery charges to Nine Elms. It was similar in all mechanical details to the 1899–1900 Dübs series, but received a truly magnificent finish with much extra lining, including the wheel centres, firebox tube inspection covers and along the sides of the boiler barrel above the sandboxes. In addition, the buffers, wheel bosses and tyres, coupling rods, window surrounds, piping, safety valve columns and cab fittings were highly burnished, while such was the quality and depth of the paint that it was December 1905 before a fresh application became necessary. As a result of its splendid external condition, it was regularly detailed for royal and other special duties. At Glasgow No 773 was displayed between Midland Railway 4-4-0 No 2591 and South Eastern & Chatham Railway 4-4-0 No 735.

Before the Dübs series entered traffic, Drummond ordered 20 further engines from Nine Elms Works at a cost of £2,210 each. They differed by having conventional fireboxes without cross water tubes, four fewer fire tubes and boilers capable of being pressed to 200lb/sq in, although in practice set to the standard 175lb working pressure. There were also minor differences to the lubrication, firebars, blast pipe and springing. Numbered 113 to 122 and 280 to 289, they entered service between June 1899 and February 1900. On test it was found that No 718 with firebox water tubes cost £41.68 more in maintenance per 35,000 miles than No 118 with a conventional firebox, but the latter burnt 8 per cent more coal and was heavier on water.

A final batch of 15 T9s, Nos 300/1/2/3/4/5/7/10/1/2/3/4/36/7/8, were ordered at a cost of £2,340 each from Nine Elms in April 1900, and delivered between December 1900 and October 1901. Two, Nos 337/8, were fitted with the Westinghouse air brake in addition to the vacuum system. There had been some criticism of the narrow cabs of the earlier engines and this Drummond answered by extending the side-

sheets of these engines to the platform edge and at the same time widening the splashers to accommodate both driving wheels and coupling rods. Firebox water tubes were carried, while the tender was of an enlarged pattern holding 4,000 gallons and with the springing and boxes concealed between the wheels and framing. Because of difficulty in riveting sections of the bottom plating these tenders always leaked to some degree, and because of this became known as Drummond watercarts. Some shed foremen were reputed to use them to lay dust and ash around their offices during periods of dry and windy weather. In 1902/07 this pattern tender became standard for the class.

At this period Drummond was experimenting with steam sanding and consequently these 15 engines were built with containers inside the smokebox with pipes leading from the sides and passing through the platform to deliver sand between the bogie wheels. There much was swept away by the elements or passage of the rear bogie wheels, while replenishing the containers through small brass-capped openings high up the smokebox sides was a task to daunt all but the most dedicated. At the first general repair, Drummond capitulated and had the containers repositioned between the frames with gravity feed to the front of the leading coupled wheels. Rearward sanding remained from a box on the right side of the tender with a narrow diameter pipe leading to the rail top.

The original drawings of these engines indicate lever reverse and water pick-up gear on the tenders, but before construction commenced steam reversing was substituted and the water

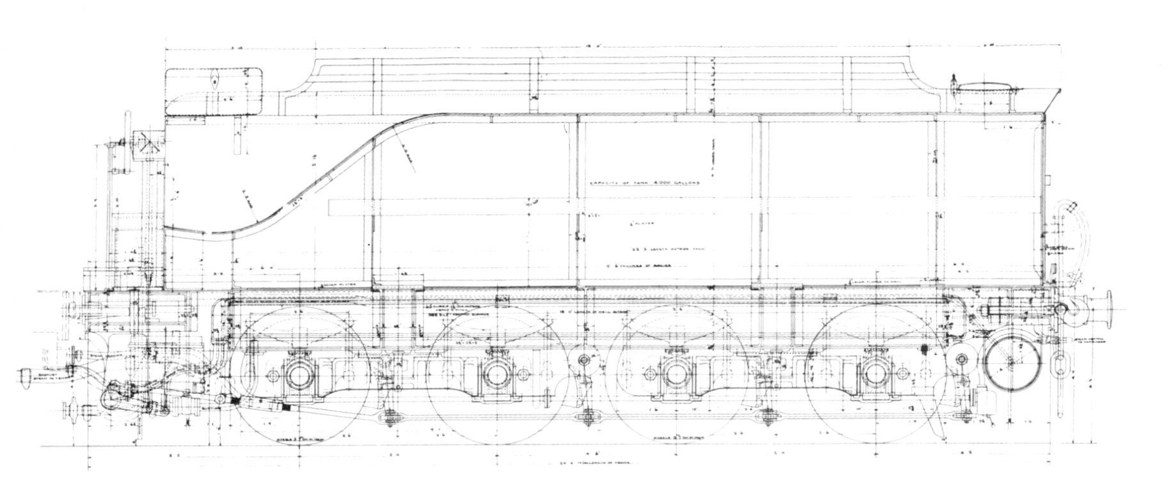

scoops omitted. Because the sand containers were sited in the smokebox, it was possible to observe the steam reverser bolted to the frames on the left side just to the front of the driving splasher. Maintenance was simpler while the absence of sand boxes on the splashers gave freer access for drivers to prepare the motion without the benefit of a pit. Many knowledgeable followers of the South Western scene always considered that this batch of T9s with their full width cabs, broad splashers, neat sanding layout and double bogie tenders were the most handsome of all the Drummond express 4-4-0s.

Like other South Western express locomotives of the period, they were painted an attractive apple green, edged with chocolate, and having an inner black line with five white lines on each side. The paint shop journal referred to these colours as royal green, purple-brown, Olympia black and Nevada white, but Drummond in correspondence described his basic livery as tartan green. All paint was prepared from ingredients in the paint shop and not purchased commercially. Drummond's formula for the apple green was four parts cypress, two parts white zinc in oil, and one part lemon chrome in

Left: No 714 in April 1902 after receiving a 4000 gallon double bogie tender.

oil, while that for the chocolate consisted of six parts of purple-brown in oil to one-quarter parts of burnt sienna and burnt umber. When fresh batches were prepared sample panels had to be painted and despatched to Drummond's office for his inspection. He was most particular about the chocolate and was known to reject two out of three samples. Indeed, on one occasion he was so exasperated by the brews prepared that he visited the paint shop and personally conducted operations. The foreman offered his resignation, only to be informed by Drummond 'not to be stupid, your work is fine, but you are colour blind where the chocolate is concerned'. With that retort he left the scene, no-one having the temerity to suggest that perhaps the boot was on the other foot.

Tenders were lettered 'LSWR' in gilt, the bright red buffer beams given gilt numerals and the cab sides provided with smooth elliptical numberplates of a pattern long associated with his Scottish engines. Round the circumference they were inscribed South Western Railway and had the numerals across the centre line. The company's coat of arms appeared on the leading splashers to complete a smart and most attractive livery. As a matter of course all engines were kept well cleaned, no difference being made whether they were intended for shunting, goods or express passenger service.

In March 1905 the cost of painting locomotives at Nine Elms was:

Type of locomotive	*Labour*	*Materials*	*Total*
Express engine and tender	£22.76	£9.00	£31.76
Mixed traffic engine and tender	18.59	7.63	26.22
Goods engine and tender	14.98	5.85	20.83
Passenger tank engine	12.40	5.58	17.98
Goods tank engine	10.63	5.11	15.74
Average cost	£22.50½		

With the 1903 S11 class mixed traffic 4-4-0s Drummond abandoned the use of numberplates in favour of transfer numerals which in time became standard for all locomotives. Despite their displacement long before collectors had entered the railway scene, a surprisingly large number of these plates remain in existence today.

Left: No 304 in April 1906 with gravity sanding and transfer numerals. The Drummond steam reverser can be seen above the centre figure.

For many years the London & South Western Railway had employed a unique locomotive classification system which was readily understandable to those familiar with its application, but somewhat confusing when met for the first time. If a class was built under contract by an outside manufacturer, then it became known by the running number of the engine first delivered. Therefore, the Neilson goods of 1881 became class 395 and the Beyer Peacock 4-4-0s of 1880 became class 135. Occasionally, if the first built engine was inconveniently numbered, then a later member was chosen as the class engine, an example being the Dübs goods of 1897 which became known as the 700s.

The same system, however, was not applied to Nine Elms built classes; in their case the engine order number was employed. Thus the 1897 double-single became T7, the 1897 0-4-4 tanks M7 and the 1898 4-4-0s C8. Again there were exceptions, usually involving a large class built under various engine orders over a period of years. Generally, though not invariably, the order of the original batch of engines was that chosen to designate the class. The 66 Drummond 4-4-0s forming the subject of this monograph were constructed under the following order numbers:

Order No	*Built by*	*Date*	*Running Nos*	*Total*
G9	Nine Elms	1899	113–22	10
K9	Nine Elms	1899/1901	280–84	5
O9	Nine Elms	1900	285–89	5
T9	Nine Elms	1900/1	300–04	5
X9	Nine Elms	1901	305/7/10/1/2	5
G10	Nine Elms	1901	313/4/36/7/8	5
	Dübs & Co	1899/1901	702–19, 721–32	30
	Dübs & Co	1901	773	1

For a time after entering traffic Nos 702–09, 721–32, and 773 were known to the men as the Dübs Express, although officially classified 702. Later, when the Nine Elms built members of the class were at work, all 66 engines were classified T9, no difference being allowed for those fitted with wider cabs, firebox water tubes, or the different pattern tenders. However, the drawing office at Nine Elms appreciated that some confusion could arise and consequently lettered the drawings T9 (Dübs), T9 (NE) and T9 (WC) to indicate the Dübs, the first Nine Elms, and wide cab varieties. To add confusion the men around

Above: K10 class (Small Hopper) 4-4-0 No 137, the mixed traffic version of the C8s.

Right: L11 class (Large Hopper) 4-4-0 No 166, the mixed traffic version of the Greyhounds.

Below: L11 class No 168 showing the Drummond 3500 gallon tender.

the same period, because of their fine turn of speed, dubbed them the Greyhounds, a nickname retained until withdrawal many years later. The terminology may have varied, but whether called T9s or Greyhounds, they were one and the same excellent class of late Victorian 4-4-0s.

To complement the small firebox C8s in the mixed traffic field, Drummond in 1901/02 introduced 40 K10 class 4-4-0s which employed the same boiler but had smaller wheels. Like the passenger series they suffered from lack of sustained power and consequently their main line use was not extensive, though they performed a useful secondary role. The South Western worked comparatively few heavy goods services, but many of a lighter nature for which six-coupled locomotives were generally unnecessary. It was also convenient for a proportion of tender stock to be capable of working slow passenger, van or pick-up goods trains, for many duties consisted of a mixture of all three and the rostering of a single locomotive avoided much unremunerative light engine running or excessive standing time. Therefore, in 1903/06, Drummond made use of the free-steaming T9 boiler for the 40 5ft 7in L11 class 4-4-0s and gained an excellent mixed traffic class which on summer Saturdays could supplement the Greyhounds on the holiday expresses. The marine type big ends of the latter seldom gave trouble in traffic, but this was not the case of the L11s in express service and because of this tendency the men never worked them to the full as they did the Greyhounds.

CHAPTER FOUR

THE GREYHOUNDS AT WORK – THE EARLY YEARS

On the Caledonian Railway, Drummond had strongly advocated the use of fully open regulators and short cut-offs when driving his express 4-4-0s. Yet, notwithstanding excellent results obtained during a series of trials, he later abandoned the scheme when he faced a dogged resistance to change by the majority of senior footplatemen. Threats, fines and suspension had no lasting effect. However, on moving south to Nine Elms the idea received a further and much more vigorous airing and in conjunction with a skilfully devised coal bonus scheme rapidly gained acceptance. Of course, some older men held fast to earlier driving methods, but by and large the South Western became cut-off conscious. This was particularly noticeable after Grouping when the new Maunsell classes entered traffic. Western Section men automatically drove them Drummond style off the reversing wheel, whereas on the Eastern and Central Sections the regulator was favoured to adjust power requirements. In practice with modern locomotives there was surprisingly little difference between the results achieved.

This was also true of the Greyhounds for they reacted well to the whims, idiosyncrasies and demands of most drivers, provided the fire was maintained deeper around the firebox walls than at the middle of the grate. There, it needed to be well covered, but with no greater depth than five to six inches and always fiercely burning. Most knowledgeable firemen followed the little and often maxim with eight to ten shovelfuls being selectively fed into the firebox at one time and the door kept closed when not in use. Coal rolled inwards and forwards with an engine's movement along the track to give a uniform thickness across the centre of the fire and to where extra coal could be added, should the appearance of holes be anticipated. Holes through the fire, diverting the passage of air from the firebed itself, rapidly caused a lowering of temperature and a drastic falling off of steam supply. Drummond was always infuriated by poor or careless firing and his manner verged on the violent should he sight any locomotive emitting clouds of black smoke. Not for him was the fireman who hurled 20 or so shovelfuls of coal into the firebox, slammed the door, turned up the blower and took a lengthy siesta. If observed by Drummond or one of his inspectors, a brief and fiery interview let the culprit know exactly what his future in railway service would be if he did not mend his ways. Few failed to change their firing technique.

As time passed and the cost of coal increased, so Drummond became acutely fuel conscious and possibly overstressed the need for economy, since most failings of his on the South Western can be traced to this overriding desire. At once there comes to mind his experiments with steam railcars and, when they proved unacceptable on country services, his move to motor trains of greater seating capacity and headed by diminutive tank locomotives. As was the intention all saved fuel, but only by severely lowering travel standards at a period when the public demanded comfort and speed on local journeys as well as on main line expresses. Like other locomotive engineers of the period, Drummond, in the changing world of transport, had to purchase experience expensively.

In June 1899, concurrently with the introduction of the Greyhounds, there was a long overdue and most necessary improvement of the Bournemouth line schedules, with the well-patronised 9am up and 4.10pm down expresses being booked non-stop over the 107½ miles between Waterloo and Bournemouth Central in 2hr 10min and 2hr 6min respectively. Over the previous 10 years traffic over this line had increased by 284 per cent and with a high proportion of first class ticket holders was rapidly becoming the most lucrative on the system. With the opening of more hotels in the area and the provision of better services, the South Western anticipated an even better future.

The engine of the 4.10pm non-stop worked right through to Weymouth and with a 7.28pm arrival gave a journey time from Waterloo of 3hr 18min. It stabled overnight at Dorchester and in the morning headed the 7.50am to Waterloo, which departed from Bournemouth Central at 9am and ran non-stop to London. On Sundays there was no through working to Weymouth, consequently on Mondays Dorchester's solitary T9, No 289, was entrusted with the duty as far as Bournemouth Central. For the remainder of the week it acted as standby for the Nine Elms engine at Dorchester and then worked the Weymouth–Bournemouth semi-fasts.

At first the formation of the two non-stop expresses was restricted to six eight-wheeled coaches of some 150 tons, but as soon as the class proved fully capable of working them without resorting to unbooked stops for water or losing time en route, the standard Bournemouth line formation of eight coaches weighing 208 tons was permitted. The tenders in general use at this period only carried 3,500 gallons and most crews were greatly relieved when the larger double bogie 4,000 gallon pattern became available. Incidentally, on several occasions Drummond attempted to install water troughs and, although having the directors' blessing, no suitable sites could be found and this useful amenity was still lacking from the London & South Western system when steam traction ceased in 1967.

The Dübs series performed much excellent work on these non-stop services and during the first month of operation No 711 ran from Bournemouth Central to Waterloo in 1hr 57¾min, including time lost by a slack before Eastleigh and a brief stop for signals at Vauxhall. The net time was probably no more than 1hr 54min with the 46¾ miles from passing Basingstoke to the signal stop being run in 45min 48 sec. The load was six bogie coaches and a van weighing 168 tons. Such running, however, was the exception rather than the rule, since signal checks and stops in the London area frequently interrupted progress and offered crews little chance of early arrivals at Waterloo. Nevertheless, time was usually kept. On the down journeys most crews found the task less exacting for any losses before Woking could easily be made good after Basingstoke and regular travellers became

Distance	*Location*	*Actual time min sec*	*Schedule*
0.0	Bournemouth Central	0.00	0.00
3.6	Christchurch	5.45	
9.4	New Milton	11.50	
12.4	Sway	14.50	
15.2	Brockenhurst	17.30	
22.6	Lyndhurst Road	24.23	
25.2	Redbridge	26.50	
28.7	Southampton West (very slow approach)	30.20	34.00
29.8	Northam Junction (10mph pw slack)	31.53	
34.4	Eastleigh	38.55	
38.2	Shawford (15mph pw slack)	43.25	
41.3	Winchester	50.55	
49.8	Micheldever	58.20	
56.0	Battledown	66.03	
60.1	Basingstoke	68.35	80.00
65.7	Hook	73.30	
68.2	Winchfield	75.50	
71.5	Fleet	79.00	
74.7	Farnborough (30mph pw slack)	82.30	
78.0	Pirbright	87.55	
79.9	Brookwood	89.30	
83.6	Woking	92.53	
86.1	Byfleet	94.58	
88.8	Weybridge	97.05	
90.8	Walton	99.00	
93.6	Esher	101.18	
95.9	Surbiton	103.33	
100.7	Wimbledon (check at Raynes Park)	108.55	
104.0	Clapham Junction (two signal checks)	113.30	123.00
106.6	Vauxhall	118.05	
107.9	Waterloo	120.45	130.00

Scheduled time: 2hr 10min
Actual time 2hr 00¾min
Net time 1hr 55min
Time gained on schedule: 15min
Load: Seven bogie coaches and one van (193 tons)
Weather: Fine, moderate side wind

Class T9 4-4-0 No 119 heads a Southampton express near Earlsfield June 1906. *Real Photographs*

so accustomed to early arrivals that grumbling occurred on those nights when correct time was kept. The recorded run (opposite) with No 703 on 17 June 1899 gives an excellent impression of the work performed daily on the 9am up express.

These services proved very popular with regular travellers and for the summer of 1900 the 12.20pm Waterloo–Bournemouth Central was also booked non-stop on Fridays and Saturdays while the 2.15pm down was rescheduled to make its first stop at Christchurch and reach Bournemouth Central in 2hr 23min. The latter was a particularly heavy train, usually loading to 10 bogies and five vans, but nevertheless gained the reputation of being the most punctual express on the line. Drummond stated at a Locomotive Committee meeting that only one late arrival had been recorded in the first three months of operation, and this on account of cattle straying along the track near New Milton. Later a new express departing Bournemouth Central at 10.30am also joined the select band of non-stops with a timing of 2hr 8min. No further major changes were made to the running times before July 1911, although the introduction of heavier electric-lighted stock made the task considerably harder. Drummond estimated that the additional resistance of this stock was the equivalent of one coach in the standard 10-coach formation. In July 1911 the 9.8am up and 4.10pm down expresses offered journey times of exactly two hours and remained the province of Nine Elms Greyhounds, despite the availability of the large L12s.

During 1900 the impact of Great Western competition for the West Country passenger traffic became more severe and in July orders were placed at Eastleigh Carriage Works for the construction of 26 bogie corridor coaches to encourage regular travellers to use the Waterloo–Exeter route. Details are: four composites (£1,050 each, 25½ tons); eight third class (£1,100, 27 tons); four second class (£1,190, 27½ tons); four first class (£1,200, 28 tons); two dining cars (£1,450, 32½ tons); and four guards vans (£480, 19½ tons). It was hoped to have them in traffic on the most popular West of England expresses by the autumn, but a belated decision to incorporate steam heating at an additional cost of £720 delayed completion until mid-December 1900. In the meantime, 10 T9s, Nos 113/9/20/1 of Nine Elms, Nos 280/2/4/5 of Salisbury, and Nos 304/5 of Exmouth Junction, had been fitted with carriage heating equipment. Trial runs were made to Exeter on 21 and 23 December 1900, and when they proved successful, the coaches were placed in regular service in the New Year on the 10.50am and 3pm down and the 12.10pm and 4.15pm up expresses.

On test it had been found that carriage heating

Greyhounds on special duty.

Above: No 729 stands at the rear of Nine Elms shed March 1907, waiting to work a royal special.

Left: No 773, the royal Greyhound, awaits the special conveying General Kitchener home from the Boer War.

Below: No 300 posed at Nine Elms for the official photographer before working the special conveying Lord Roberts from Southampton to Waterloo.

increased the fuel consumption by six ounces of coal per vehicle mile. This, when all the company's rolling stock had been similarly equipped, would have required an additional 6,052 tons of coal annually, and at £0.77 per ton, increased the running costs by £4,705. Some directors found this extortionate and questioned the necessity of providing such luxurious travel; therefore, in January 1902 Drummond was instructed to investigate means of reducing the cost of carriage heating. Over a four-week period the engines of four selected expresses had their coal consumption measured while the heating equipment was in use, the findings being recorded and later compared with figures obtained from the same services in May 1902 when the weather was warmer and carriage heating could be dispensed with. To the surprise of all concerned the difference between the findings was much less than had been supposed, for the original assessment had taken insufficient account of the human element, in particular the ingenuity shown by crews in making life on the footplate as pleasant as circumstances permitted. Apparently, it had become standard practice to heat trains thoroughly before journeys commenced, since it was then that steam generated by the boiler was being put to no practical use and was in danger of being lost via the safety valves. At the right-away the heating was reduced to a minimum or even turned off and only re-employed when running down banks or when steam was in abundance. Under these circumstances the additional cost per annum was reassessed at £1,260, a figure the directors found acceptable and by 31 December 1906 all South Western coaches possessed steam heating.

At this period the best West of England expresses took 3hr 35min and 5hr 44min to reach Exeter and Plymouth Friary respectively:

DOWN

10.50am Waterloo–Exeter	2.25pm.	Time 3h 35m, stops 10min
11.00am ,, ,,	2.57pm.	Time 3h 57m, stops 18min
3.00pm ,, ,,	6.45pm.	Time 3h 45m, stops 13min
5.50pm ,, ,,	10.05pm.	Time 4h 15m, stops 27min
10.50am Waterloo–Plymouth	4.34pm.	Time 5h 44m, stops 37min

UP

10.20am Exeter–Waterloo	2.40pm.	Time 4h 20m, stops 28min
12.00pm ,, ,,	3.40pm.	Time 3h 40m, stops 10min
12.40pm ,, ,,	5.00pm.	Time 4h 20m, stops 22min
4.15pm ,, ,,	8.21pm.	Time 4h 06m, stops 24min
9.55am Plymouth–Waterloo	3.40pm.	Time 5h 45m, stops 31min

The Great Western was still running its Plymouth services via Swindon and Bristol, but nevertheless the best were about 25min swifter than the South Western:

10.35am Paddington–Plymouth 3.53pm. Time 5hr 18min
10.30am Plymouth–Paddington 3.50pm. Time 5hr 20min

Obviously with even quicker timings in the offing with the pending completion of the through Berks & Hants route, the Great Western was strongly positioned, hence the trepidation felt at Waterloo.

On the South Western it was standard practice to change engines at Salisbury and Exeter on the Plymouth expresses with as long as 10min being allowed for the operation at the former and 12min at the last-mentioned station. In fact, much less time was necessary and over the next few years these periods were progressively reduced until 5min became the average. Swift action was then essential and the Salisbury changeover always gathered a small band of interested travellers much intrigued by the well-drilled and deft movements of the staff and locomotives. Despite the speed of events, most drivers still found time to have a last oil round. For the summer months of 1901 Nine Elms and Exmouth Junction sheds broke with tradition and worked engines throughout between Waterloo and Exeter, but, when the winter services recommenced, a return was made to the Salisbury exchanges. Later in the summer of 1904 through engine workings were instigated between Plymouth and Templecombe, but this, too, was abandoned in the autumn.

A typical run by No 287 with the 3.30pm Waterloo–Exeter loaded to 254 tons gave the following timing:

Distance	*Location*	*Actual time min/sec*	*Schedule*
0.0	Waterloo	0.00	0.00
1.3	Vauxhall	3.07	
3.9	Clapham Junction	6.22	7.00
7.2	Wimbledon	10.17	
12.0	Surbiton	15.14	
14.3	Esher (signal checks)		
19.1	Weybridge	22.18	
24.3	Woking	27.36	
28.0	Brookwood	31.36	
31.0	Milepost 31	35.15	
33.2	Farnborough	37.33	
42.2	Hook	46.31	
47.8	Basingstoke	52.00	57.00
50.3	Worting Junction	54.52	
52.4	Oakley	57.24	
55.6	Overton	60.46	
59.2	Whitchurch	64.08	
61.1	Hurstbourne	65.50	
66.4	Andover Junction	70.29	76.00
72.8	Grateley	77.29	
78.3	Porton	83.32	
82.7	Tunnel Junction	87.20	
83.8	Salisbury	89.26	94.00

Above No 715 passes Earlsfield in September 1900, the signalman showing greater interest in the photographer than the express.

Scheduled time: 94min
Actual time: 89½min
Net time: 88 min
Time gained on schedule: 6min
Weather: Fine, slight westerly wind

SPEEDS:

Maximum to Weybridge:	63mph
At Milepost 31:	50½mph
Maximum to Basingstoke:	64mph
At Battledown:	49mph
At Andover Junction:	68½mph
At Grateley:	44½mph
At Porton:	68mph

It was a good steady journey with no great acceleration out of Waterloo or particularly high speeds, but No 287 at all times was master of its

Below: A down Bournemouth express with No 307 in charge September 1907. *[Locomotive Publishing Co*

task and gradually gained on schedule until by Basingstoke the driver was more interested in spinning out time before the Salisbury stop than in fast running. At Salisbury No 287 retired to the shed and was replaced by No 113 which with two extra coaches passed Yeovil Junction in 40min 37sec (schedule 42), Axminster in 64min 56sec (schedule 67), and reached Exeter in 93min 24sec, as against the 96 minutes scheduled.

Another smart run was recorded by No 773 on 21 February 1902 when rostered for an up Union Boat express:

Distance	Location	Actual time min/sec
0.0	Shawford (pass)	0.00
3.1	Winchester	5.02
5.2	Winchester Junction	7.29
7.9	Waller's Ash East	10.26
11.6	Micheldever	14.31
13.5	Litchfield Box	16.38
19.4	Worting Junction	22.38
21.9	Basingstoke (pass)	24.49

SPEEDS:
At Winchester: 52mph
At Winchester Junction: 56mph
At Micheldever: 53½mph
At Basingstoke: 80mph

The load was moderate, only three first class bogie coaches, a kitchen car and two luggage vans, but nevertheless the passage up through Winchester was excellent and suggested that the class was equally happy climbing banks as running down them.

During the first decade of the 20th century the company's working timetable continued to be compiled on the assumption that most main line passenger and goods duties would commence and terminate in the London area. Consequently a high proportion of the locomotive stock was concentrated at Nine Elms (253) and Strawberry Hill (124). The total number of locomotives in service on 1 October 1903 was:

Express passenger tender	192
Mixed traffic tender	154
Goods tender	149
Passenger tank	268
Goods tank	86
	849

This concentration of motive power around London naturally led to much unproductive time being spent at country depots awaiting suitable return workings or the amassing of excessive and expensive light engine mileages. The former is well illustrated in a report made by Drummond to the Locomotive Committee in April 1904.

Train	Class	Working time* Down	Working time* Up	Miles worked	Idle time*	Days work*
12.30pm Waterloo–Bournemouth West	T9	2.53	2.24	222½	2.03	5.17
11.00am Waterloo–Salisbury	T9	1.31	1.32	167½	1.14	3.03
9.10am Waterloo–Portsmouth	T9	2.00	2.03	148½	3.35	4.03

* *Hr/min*

The Portsmouth line engine spent almost the same time on shed during the day as at work.

The Greyhound allocation for October 1903 showed the same concentration: Nine Elms Nos 113–21, 300/1/2/3, 702/3/4/5/11/2/8/9/28/73; Strawberry Hill Nos 286/7; Basingstoke Nos 307/10; Guildford Nos 708/16; Eastleigh Nos 311/2/3, 710/7; Salisbury Nos 422, 280/1/2/4/5; Bournemouth Nos 314, 721/2/3/9; Portsmouth Nos 336/7/8; Dorchester No 287; Yeovil Nos 713/4; Exmouth Junction Nos 304/5, 706/7/9/15; Plymouth No 288.

After the new running shed at Eastleigh opened in January 1903 and the yards were extended in 1904/07 at Salisbury, Bournemouth and Guildford, more locomotives were stationed away from London with corresponding improvement in daily train mileages, although it was left to Robert Urie in 1913/14 to introduce a truly practical working timetable.

An unexpected bonus followed this transfer to the country depots for it brought a welcome reduction in maintenance costs, since it proved cheaper to service locomotives away from London as well as offering better availability:

AVERAGE YEARLY COST

Depot	Approximate allocation	Type of locomotive: Tender	Type of locomotive: Tank
		£	£
Nine Elms	240	677	402
Eastleigh	220	516	327
Bournemouth	50	483	296
Salisbury	70	426	193
Exmouth Junction	90	404	187
Wimborne	12	239	154
Yeovil	15	243	161

The costs included those incurred maintaining and cleaning locomotives as well as those of materials, machinery, building and turntable maintenance, rates and main services, but not that of coal, oil and sand.

The South Western was always very price conscious and under Drummond's superintendency Nine Elms was building and repairing locomotives more cheaply than most other railways.

BUILDING COSTS

Railway	Works	Type	Class	Date	Cost
					£
LSWR	Nine Elms	4-4-0	T9	1899	2,210
LSWR	Nine Elms	4-4-0	T9	1901	2,340
LSWR	Nine Elms	4-4-0	S11	1903	2,435
LC&DR	Longhedge	4-4-0	M3	1898/99	2,951
SE&CR	Ashford	0-6-0	C	1903	2,165
SE&CR	Ashford	4-4-0	D	1901	2,390
LB&SCR	Brighton	4-4-0	B4	1900	3,255
Midland	Derby	4-4-0	S&DJR	1900	3,500
Caledonian	St Rollox	4-4-0	900	1900	3,049
L&YR	Horwich	4-4-2	Atlantic	1899	3,480

REPAIR COSTS – T9 CLASS 1904 TO 1908

Engine No	1904	1905	1906	1907	1908	Total
	£	£	£	£	£	£
718	199	108	64	34	680*	1,385
723	32	33	230	128	236	659
724	186	14	69	314	53	636
732	227	120	9	287	193	838
773	23	306	16	411	19	765

** New boiler fitted*

The average cost of repairs at Nine Elms Works during this period for the entire class was £584, which compared most favourably with those of similar locomotives working on the South Eastern & Chatham and London Brighton & South Coast Railways, details being as follows:

WORKSHOP REPAIR COSTS 1904 TO 1908

Railway	Class	
		£
LSWR	T9	584
LSWR	S11	683
LSWR	L12	634
SE&CR	M3	809
SE&CR	D	814
SE&CR	E	877
LB&SCR	B4	912

Like most railways at the period, South Western locomotives as a general rule retained their own boilers, but in 1907 a noteworthy development was the establishment of an interchange system with the intention of reducing the time spent under repair at Nine Elms. Under normal circumstances a locomotive boiler took longer to overhaul than the frames, wheels, cylinders, etc, therefore, time was invariably lost in the erecting shop awaiting the return of this vital part. A float of spare boilers would avoid this and also ensure that the erecting shop staff was always gainfully employed and not changing from one job to another during the working

Below left: A boat express for a North German Lloyd liner at Earlsfield headed by No 714 in November 1910. 1910.

Above: No. 721 approaches Vauxhall with the 12.50pm Waterloo–Portsmouth on 27 March 1909.
[Ken Nunn/Locomotive Club of Great Britain

day. To this end in 1907 a number of boilers of varying sizes were built at Nine Elms; two for the T9s were fitted to Nos 303 and 718 at a cost of £548 each, while the discarded boilers were repaired and placed in the spares pool awaiting the next member of the class entering works for heavy boiler or firebox attention.

An added complication was the existence of two types of firebox on the class, those carried by Nos 113–22 and 280–89 being of conventional pattern, whereas those fitted to the others had the added complication of cross water tubes. Drummond stubbornly refused to permit the transfer of boilers with firebox water tubes to locomotives not already possessing the feature, therefore to some degree the erecting shop delays persisted until the opening of the new repair shop at Eastleigh. Then Robert Urie ordered six more boilers, without firebox water tubes, and in 1913 fitted them to Nos 303, 713/4/21/8/32, while at the same time instigating a policy of removing the firebox water tubes from the older boilers as and when heavy repairs became necessary.

It will be recalled that during his Caledonian superintendency Drummond had investigated the merits of high boiler pressure and expansive working, and, although the findings were reasonably conclusive, once more, in October 1905, he commenced a series of trials. No 305 was the engine chosen and on various occasions during that month worked 10-coach specials between Clapham Yard and Brockenhurst, the working pressure ranging from the standard 175lb to 210lb/sq in. The following is a selection of performance with the higher pressure:

Cut off per cent	*Boiler pressure lb/sq in*	*Steam chest pressure lb/sq in*	*Regulator opening per cent*	*Speed mph*	*Indicated horse power*
70	210	175	50	10½	448
55	210	193	70	21	720
40	204	196	100	38	913
37	201	195	100	43	1,018
30	198	193	100	62	925
27	203	194	100	71	964
27	208	194	100	64	931
27	206	195	100	54	869

Coal burnt per train mile (best Welsh) : 33.26lb
Weather: Dry, no wind
Train: Nine bogie coaches and a bogie guards van

Some trouble appears to have been met in maintaining the high working pressure, but no problems arose with the fast non-stop schedules. The ihp readings were good for a moderately sized 4-4-0 employing saturated steam. After the trials No 305 reverted to the standard 175lb working pressure before returning to regular traffic.

During the early years of the century the Greyhounds gained an enviable reputation for

speed, ease of maintenance and reliability. They were well-liked by the men who, with regular engines, obtained the best possible work from them by ensuring they were always in first rate mechanical order and driven with skill and understanding. Because of restricted lubrication the marine type big ends were susceptible to prolonged thrashing or violent acceleration, although otherwise withstanding the trepidations of railway service exceptionally well. Aware of this, drivers developed the technique of accelerating steadily from stops and only fully opening up when well under way, while lost time was usually regained by employing the free-steaming boiler to best advantage for fast running both uphill and down. Mile after mile could be run at speeds between 75 and 85mph with little apparent effort or strain. There were, however, limitations and once they had been reached few drivers were prepared to press on regardless and accept the consequences. Fortunately, the standard of performance was such that the point of no return was seldom reached and drivers were saved from dire decisions. The outside cylinder Adams 4-4-0s could be thrashed unmercifully and carry on working, the Drummonds could not. The average period between general repairs in 1903/08 was 22 months, and the mileage 63,460, figures which could not be bettered by any other South Western class and in the south of England were only equalled by the South Eastern & Chatham D class 4-4-0s. The South Western main line without a preponderance of Greyhounds on the express services was just inconceivable.

Above: Even the Greyhounds sometimes suffered the indignity of hot boxes; No 706 is lifted at Nine Elms shed August 1902.

Below: Outlined against the sky No 716 approaches Clapham Cutting with an up excursion from Bournemouth. *[Real Photographs*

CHAPTER FIVE

THE DRUMMOND FINALE

The steep gradients and difficult working conditions of the Salisbury–Exeter line naturally influenced the type of express locomotives provided for these services by successive London & South Western mechanical engineers. Beset by the problem in the early days of steam locomotion, Joseph Beattie introduced several classes of 2-4-0 having 6ft driving wheels, but otherwise being of similar boiler and cylinder capacity to larger wheeled engines of the type employed on the easier graded Waterloo–Southampton and Basingstoke–Salisbury lines. This policy evidently fulfilled its object for it became traditional to build smaller wheeled express locomotives for service west of Salisbury. William Adams introduced several classes of 4-4-0 with 6ft 7in and 7ft 1in coupled wheels; the former were found all over the system, but those carrying the larger wheels seldom ventured past Salisbury.

At first Drummond saw no reason to maintain this practice and daily rostered his Greyhounds for the Portsmouth, Bournemouth and West of England expresses, but later he too was persuaded to conform and in March 1903 ordered 10 4-4-0s with 6ft 1in driving wheels from Nine Elms Works at a cost of £2,435 each. Known as the S11 class and numbered 395 to 404, they were completed before the end of the year when they were seen to be Greyhounds of the final 300 series fitted with smaller wheels, 19in cylinders and 5ft diameter boilers. There was no change of grate area or working pressure, although the crank axle was of steel with the webs extended to counterbalance the crank pins and obviate the need for driving wheel balance weights. This axle was a Drummond patent and had been carried experimentally by Nos 281, 305 and 724 in 1901/03, but the S11s were the first new locomotives to be equipped.

The intention was to employ the new class on the Plymouth Ocean Liner specials which ran in competition with the Great Western Railway and all 10 initially were stationed in the West Country. Time, however, proved that their smaller wheels, 19in cylinders and larger boilers offered little positive advantage over the Greyhounds, for most crews found the smaller engines equally capable on the banks and considerably faster on the down grades and level stretches of line. The Greyhounds were also easier on water, an important factor on a railway devoid of track troughs, while the higher pitched boiler of the S11s so adversely affected the riding that few drivers were prepared to approach junctions or speed restrictions with quite the gay abandon adopted with their predecessors. Nevertheless, the S11s with their well-designed front end, generous bearing surfaces and robust construction proved an asset to the South Western until the advent of the Urie N15 class 4-6-0s in 1918/23.

To complement the class on the Bournemouth services and those between Waterloo and Salisbury, Drummond in 1904/05 built 20 similar 4-4-0s with 6ft 7in coupled wheels. They, too, proved useful additions to the company's express stock, but again seldom showing much advance on the Greyhounds. Numbered 415 to 434 and classified L12, they were shared when new between the running sheds of Nine Elms, Bournemouth and Salisbury, but later Nos 427/8 were transferred to Exmouth Junction where they joined S11s Nos 395/6/7/8, 403 in the top link.

The London & South Western American Ocean Liner specials from Plymouth first ran in May 1903, although it was 9 April 1904 before they operated on a weekly basis. A loosely worded agreement was in force with the Great Western under which the South Western took charge of the trans-Atlantic passengers while the former, with equal alacrity, conveyed the mails to Paddington. Following the abolition of the broad gauge, the Great Western had slowly emerged from a lengthy hibernation and by the opening years of the 20th century was operating some of the fastest passenger services in the country. Consequently, in 1904 the South Western at Plymouth was facing ever increasing competition as well as being threatened by the shortening of its rival's route to the West Country. When the Castle Cary–Langport cut-off was opened the South Western, already beset by a more difficult road, would also have to contend with a sizeable mileage disadvantage. All drivers regularly rostered for the Ocean Liner specials were personally briefed by Drummond and instructed to keep time, bearing in mind weather conditions and speed restrictions. Signalmen were similarly ordered to give these expresses precedence over all other services.

The booking was non-stop from Devonport to Waterloo, though in reality a stop was made at Templecombe to exchange engines, while the Great Western frequently exercised its right to hold South Western services momentarily at St David's, Exeter. Very fast running was the rule and, as early as 20 April 1904 the passage of Salisbury station was causing concern and drivers had been warned to restrict their speed to 30mph, but apparently with little effect, for the instruction was repeated on 3 May and again more forcefully on 16 June 1904. Later the schedule was revised to give an extra minute between Templecombe and Hampton Court Junction to encourage the Salisbury slowing.

This then was the position on the fatal night of 30 June 1906, when the special departed from Stonehouse Pool with passengers from RMS *New York*. It consisted of a brake van, three first class saloons and a kitchen car/brake with a net weight of 113 tons, and was worked from Devonport by No 288 in grand style to reach Templecombe one minute early, where L12 No

Right: Large Drummond 6ft 7in L12 class 4-4-0 No 417 in September 1904.

Below: Fig 11 General arrangement drawing of the Drummond 1904/5 L12 class 4-4-0. *[British Railways*

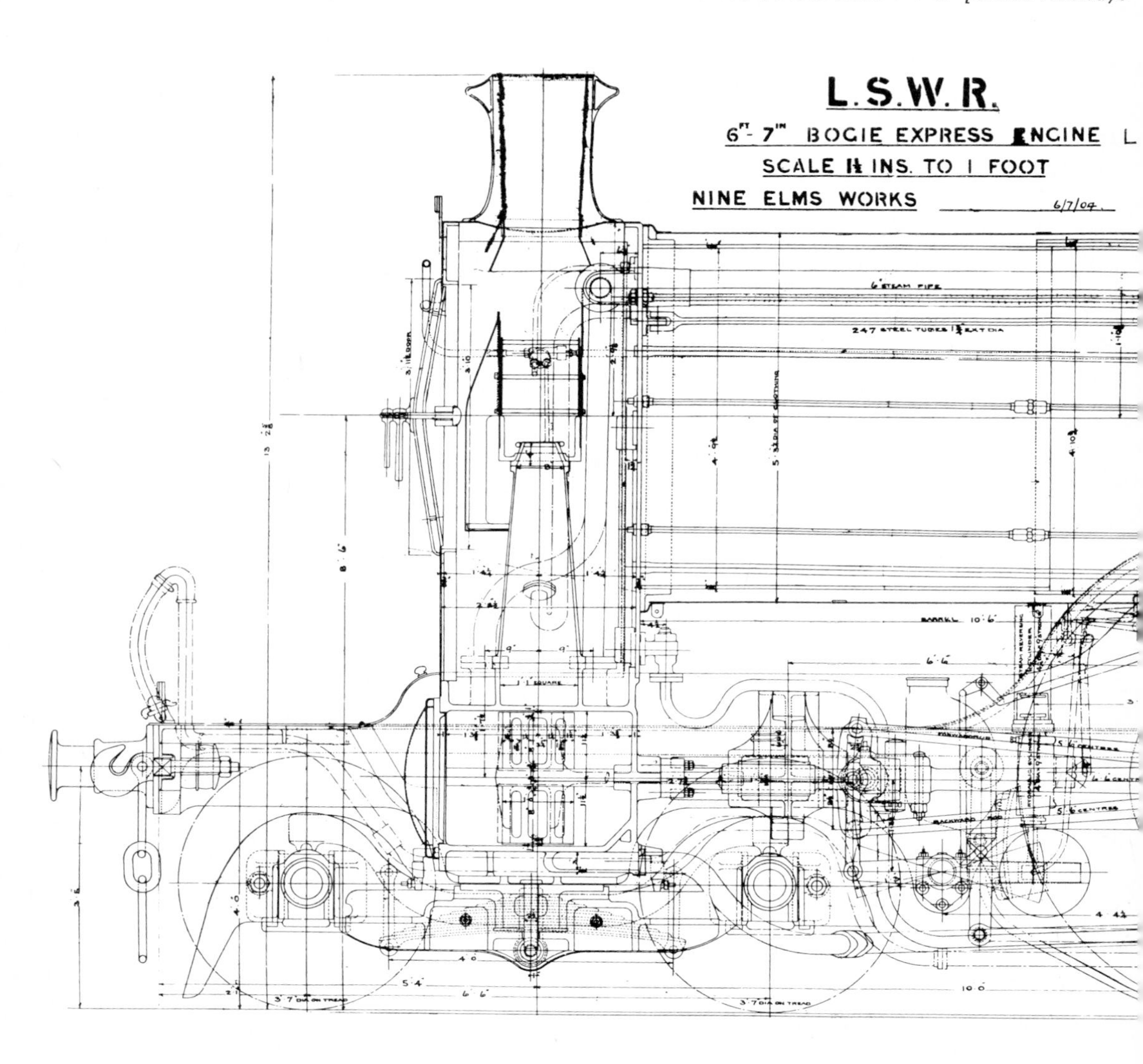

417
L S W R

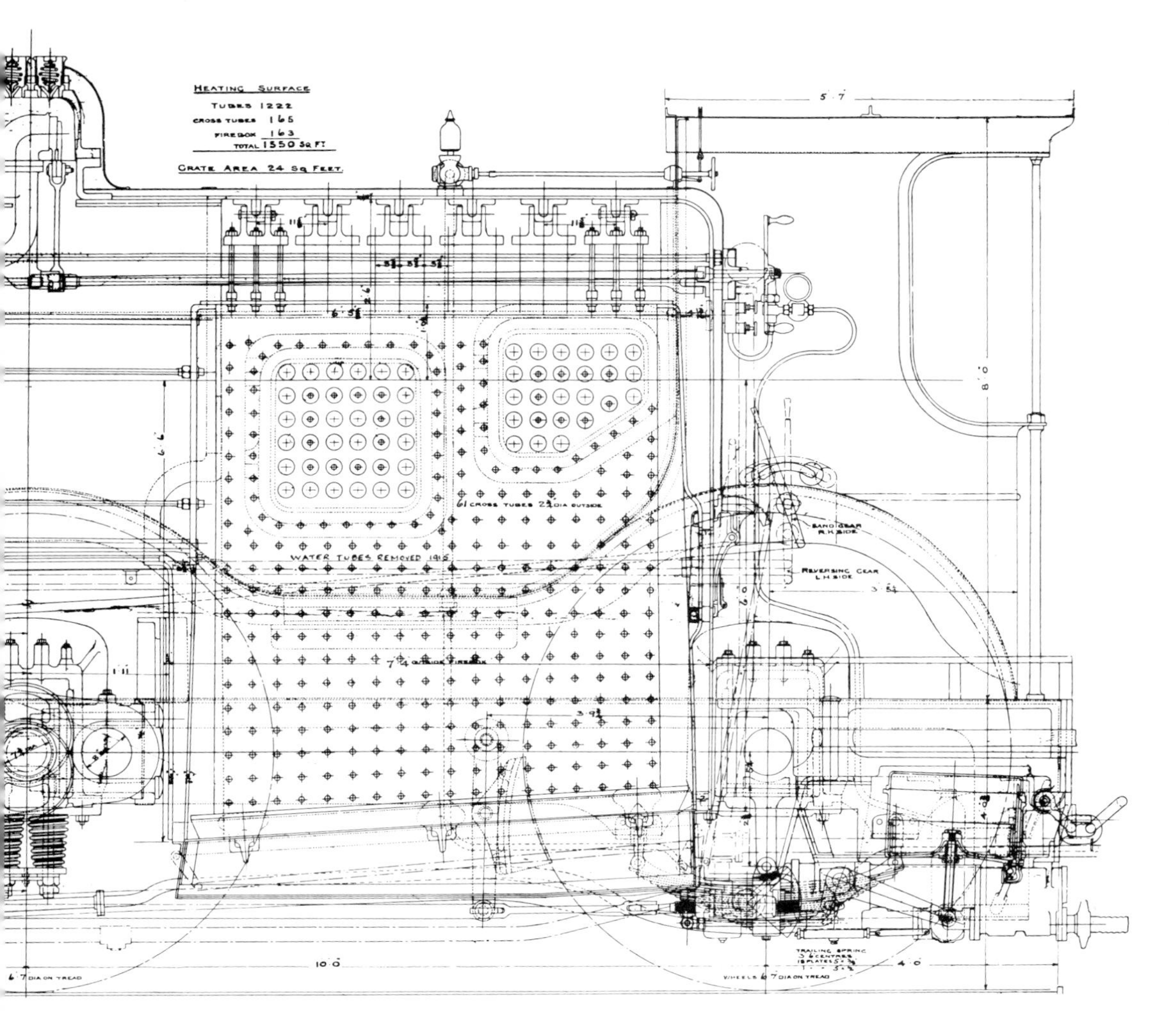
HEATING SURFACE
TUBES 1222
CROSS TUBES 165
FIREBOX 163
TOTAL 1550 SQ FT
GRATE AREA 24 SQ FEET.
61 CROSS TUBES 2¾ DIA OUTSIDE
WATER TUBES REMOVED 1915
SAND GEAR R.H. SIDE
REVERSING GEAR L.H. SIDE
TRAILING SPRING
3 6 CENTRES
WHEELS 6 7 DIA ON TREAD
6 7 DIA ON TREAD
10 0
4 0
5 7

The first London & South Western six-coupled express locomotive, F13 class No 330 in September 1905.

421 took over for the run to Waterloo. The start was unusually slow, but speed thereafter increased, with Dinton being passed at 70mph and the same speed maintained through Wilton. So far there was no cause for the guard to show alarm, but there was most certainly at the approach to Salisbury where the up distant was passed with scant reduction in speed and no brake application made. The platform road was rushed at 55mph and at the sharp curve before Fisherton Street bridge No 421 listed so far over that it struck another train and left the rails. Damage to the stock, lineside buildings and passengers was severe with 24 dead plus the crew. At the subsequent inquiry Drummond spoke dramatically of finding the L12s regulator closed, the vacuum brake handle in the running position and the reversing gear in forward gear. Various theories were offered for the driver's behaviour, but all lacked authenticity and the inquiry closed on an unsatisfactory note. In Drummond's personal report of the incident to the directors he stated with characteristic bluntness 'lack of care by driver and excessive speed approaching Salisbury' – which, if not explaining the accident, at least agreed with all known facts.

By March 1905, with over a hundred modern and capable express 4-4-0s in traffic, the South Western was well provided with motive power. Nevertheless, Drummond was not prepared to rest on his laurels, for he appreciated that the next decade would bring not only higher speeds but the introduction of heavier and more resistant electrically-lit stock. Of necessity engines would have to work considerably harder, and, as willing as his 4-4-0s might be, he rightly perceived that they could not be expected to contend adequately with both demands, especially over the switchback main line west of Salisbury. Consequently with some reluctance he transferred his allegiance from modestly proportioned 4-4-0s to large four-cylinder 4-6-0s, five of which, F13 class Nos 330–34, entered traffic from Nine Elms Works towards the end of 1905.

In all respects their construction was massive with 6ft coupled wheels, four 16in × 24in cylinders, 5ft 6in diameter boiler, a grate area of 31½sq ft and a weight in working order of 76¾ tons. The cylinder layout followed that of the 1901 double-singles in which the inside pair, with divided ports and valves between, were conventionally positioned abreast the smokebox while the outside cylinders were mounted to the fore of the leading coupled wheels and had their valves below. Stephenson motion was provided for the inside cylinders and Walschaerts for the outside. A sixth and slightly modified 4-6-0, E14 class No 335, followed in 1907, which used the same boiler, frames and wheels, but had the cylinders enlarged to 16½in × 26in with the design of the outer pair modified to accept piston valves.

Unfortunately in express service both series proved abject failures for they were plagued from the very outset by hot boxes, poor steaming and an aversion to fast running. The shallow firebox called for an entirely different technique from that employed with such success on the Greyhounds and few firemen appeared able or willing to learn it. Most coal had to be fired immediately below the door and left to vibration for distribution down the grate, but great care and skill was also necessary to keep the back of the fire burning fiercely. Should this be otherwise, then the entire grate rapidly turned to clinker, lost its capacity for generating heat, and placed the crew in serious trouble, since control of the fire once lost could not be regained at the head of an express. Unusually for Drummond sufficient care had not been taken to ensure that adequate bearing surfaces were provided for the coupled boxes and all six engines suffered accordingly. Before long they were surreptitiously removed from passenger service and relegated to the West of England goods and Salisbury–Southampton coal trains where they proved much more successful, to such an extent that the six 0-8-0s using the same boiler and having four 16½in × 26in cylinders, ordered for these services were no longer required and could be cancelled. Nos 330–34 were withdrawn by the Southern Railway in 1924 while No 335 was rebuilt by Robert Urie in 1914 as a two-cylinder H15 class mixed traffic 4-6-0.

All mechanical engineers have their disappointments and Drummond had his share, although lack of courage and determination could not be listed amongst his failings. Therefore, despite his disheartening venture into the six-coupled field, he at once returned to the drawing board and in 1908 was back with G14 class Nos 453–57. They were smaller locomotives with four 15in × 26in cylinders, 4ft 11in diameter boiler, 31½sq ft grate, 6ft coupled wheels and a weight in working order of 71 tons. Generally the front end layout followed that of No 335 with Walschaerts gear driving the piston valves of the outside cylinders and Stephenson the slide valves of the inside pair. Like the earlier 4-6-0s the safety valves were positioned over the firebox while an interesting extra was a steam drier consisting of a number of small diameter tubes joining headers at the smokebox top to similar fittings at the base. This remarkable device was Drummond's answer to the superheater currently coming into use on other railways, notably the Great Western and the London Brighton & South Coast, a contraption he considered expensive to fit and maintain as well as being an unnecessary smokebox complication. His intention was to employ the heat of the exhaust gases to dry but not greatly to raise the temperature of the steam during its passage to the cylinders and by so doing to increase its capacity for work. The drier was certainly of simple, robust and unobtrusive construction, but unhappily in service it had little effect on performance or fuel consumption and must be considered another of the designer's ideas which expressed much inventiveness, yet had little practical value.

When completed between March and May 1908, Nos 453–57 were set to work on the Salisbury–Exeter expresses and at once proved more successful than the earlier 4-6-0s. When skilfully fired and judiciously driven over this difficult line their performance was superior to the 4-4-0s, but should control of the fire be forfeited then time was invariably lost. More coal was burnt for equal work while the maintenance and repair costs for 1910/14 averaged 28 per cent more than the Greyhounds. Perusal of the Fines Register (black book) suggests that Salisbury men had a better understanding of their foibles than most, since their names seldom appear accused of lost time, but numerous are the fines imposed on Exmouth Junction and Nine Elms crews.

Drummond was reasonably pleased with their performance and in February 1909 ordered five more, P14 class Nos 448–52, but their construction was severely delayed by the transfer of the company's locomotive workshops from Nine Elms to Eastleigh, and it was not until February 1911 before the last entered traffic. Costs of the various Drummond 4-6-0s were: F13 (Nos 330–34) £3,100; E14 (No 335) £3,799; G14 (Nos 453–57) £3,260; P14 (Nos 448–52) £3,160.

Generally the 1910/11 series followed the G14s, although differing by having piston valves to all cylinders, a longer coupled wheelbase, enlarged steam drier and a weight of 74¾ tons. All went to Exmouth Junction shed for service on the Salisbury expresses and when resolutely driven and fired gave a good account of themselves with a reasonable turn of speed considering their 6ft drivers. Like Nos 453–57, they remained on the West of England trains until relieved by the Urie N15 class 4-6-0s after the first world war, when all 10 engines were relegated to secondary duties until withdrawn by the Southern Railway in 1925/27. Their tenders, however, lived on and saw long service behind King Arthurs Nos 448–57, built at Eastleigh Works in 1925.

L S W R
445
L S W R

458
L S W R

Above: T14 class 4-6-0 No 443 leaves Waterloo with the 2.00pm Bournemouth express on 16 May 1912.
[Ken Nunn/Locomotive Club of Great Britain

Top left: Drummond inspects his latest masterpiece, P14 class 4-6-0 No 448 at Eastleigh Works, October 1910.

Centre left: T14 class (Double-Breaster) 4-6-0 No 445 outside Eastleigh Works, 8 September 1911.

Bottom left: A superheated Drummond 4-6-0, T14 class No 458, March 1918.

All the Drummond 4-6-0s so far described were built for the Salisbury–Exeter expresses and because of this were provided with smaller driving wheels. However, in July 1910, it was the turn of the more easily graded Bournemouth line when Drummond ordered five 4-6-0s with 6ft 7in coupled wheels. Numbered 443–47 and classified T14, they were completed by Eastleigh Works at a cost of £3,125 each between March and June 1911. The boilers were based on those carried by classes G14 and P14, although appearing larger because of the higher pitching in the frames and the shorter mountings. There was no change of grate area, but the working pressure was increased to 200lb/sq in. Although of the same size, the cylinders differed in layout, for the outside pair were moved forward to bring all four in line below the smokebox. The running plate was straight and level with the top of the buffer beam, as in the previous 4-6-0s, but the piston valves of the outside cylinders were above the platform. A large casing joined the cylinders to the smokebox giving the class an unusually massive appearance when viewed from the leading end – which gave rise to one of their nicknames, 'the Double Breasters'. The other arose from the enormous splashers which covered both the coupled wheels and the outside valves, and by conjuring up thoughts of holiday trips abroad, paddle steamers suggested the alternative sobriquet of 'Paddleboxes'. The outside valve gear passed through the splasher fronts to reach the piston valves, while, unlike the earlier 4-6-0s, the inside piston valves were operated by rocking levers connected to the outside gear.

Five similar engines, Nos 458–62, were constructed at a cost of £3,060 each between December 1911 and April 1912. All had steam driers, whereas only No 447 of the 1911 series was equipped. The 10 T14s were easily the best Drummond 4-6-0s and successfully worked the Bournemouth expresses until after the first world war. When tried over the Salisbury–Exeter line their performance was less impressive and consequently the class was normally restricted to service east of Salisbury. Hot boxes also proved a constant source of trouble, although this apparently did not seriously affect their yearly mileages for all ran over a million miles before withdrawal in 1940/51. The first to go, No 458, was a victim of a German air attack on London when it was so badly damaged that repair was not considered worth the expense.

Very shortly an accident was to remove Drummond from office, but, blissfully unaware of what fate had in store, he busied himself

The final Drummond 4-4-0 design, D15 class No 466 in July 1912.

during the summer and autumn of 1911 preparing drawings of yet another express design. More 4-6-0s were confidently anticipated, but to everyone's surprise a return was made to the four-coupled type. Classified D15 and completed between February and December 1912 by Eastleigh Works at a cost of £2,700 each, they were a studied and skilful enlargement of his standard express 4-4-0. The main problem facing Drummond was the incorporation of 19½in cylinders, piston valves and a 5ft diameter boiler without upsetting the general pattern, and at the same time retaining ample bearing surfaces. He was fully conversant with the evils of gaining space by cramping parts together and most wisely discarded any earlier concepts which could not be enlarged without loss of efficiency. Therefore, when it proved quite impracticable to fit 19½in cylinders and 10in piston valves and to retain the steam chests between the cylinders, he repositioned them above where ample space was available, while to ensure good bearing surfaces, Walschaerts valve gear was substituted for the Stephenson motion. By so doing, of course, the number of eccentrics was halved and with the cylinders at 22in centres there was space for 5in crank webs and 9in main bearings. The crank axle was balanced, while the Walschaerts valve gear was exceptionally sturdy and had several interesting features, for the eccentric rods were not attached as normal to the expansion links, but worked off drop arms from short rocking shafts, at the outer extremities of which the links were joined. The motion, therefore, was transferred from the plane of the eccentrics to that of the valves without the necessity of 'donkey legs'. The motion plate remained at the centre of the slide bars, but because the crosshead arm of the Walschaerts motion depended on the face of the crosshead, the usual Drummond trough bars could not be employed and they were of the two-bar type. Large valve spindle bearings were housed in pedestals cast in the top of the motion plate, while the radius arms were divided to embrace these bearings. Outside admission was provided for the piston valves with free exhaust to the blast pipes.

The engine wheelbase was 6ft 6in + 8ft 3in + 10ft = 24ft 9in, 18in more than the T9s, S11s and L12s from the rear of the bogie to the driving wheels. To allow for this, the connecting rods were lengthened from the standard 6ft 6in to 7ft while the coupling rods were fluted. The boiler was based on that fitted to double-single No 720 in March 1905 and when the firebox proved over-long to drop between the coupled axles, Drummond pitched it higher in the frames and sloped the grate to clear the trailing axle. Designers of direct stayed fireboxes usually arranged for the first two or three rows of the front roof stays to be slung from the wrapper plate in order to offer a degree of flexibility to the tube plate and front of the firebox roof. Drummond, however, in his larger fireboxes went further and fitted slung stays to the entire roof to gain even greater flexibility. Since the D15 firebox gave little trouble and on the average worked higher mileages than those carried by the T9s it appears that Drummond's thinking was sound. Like most engines built latterly for the South Western they carried feed water heaters which took the form of 65 × 1¼in diameter tubes with a heating surface of 382sq ft positioned in the tender well. Boiler feed was by two duplex pumps bolted to the frames on either side between the coupled wheels. After favouring injectors for some years Drummond rejected them and employed pumps on his later engines. In addition, the usual cross firebox water tubes and steam drier were fitted.

In traffic the D15s performed exceptionally well and at once took their share of the Bournemouth expresses in turn with the T14s. Many crews preferred them to the 4-6-0s, finding them easier on fuel, water and oil, as well as being simpler to prepare and put away.

After the embarrassment of his earlier 4-6-0s, Drummond must have been delighted with their performance, although he was not granted long to savour his success for he died in November 1912 before the last member of the class entered traffic.

Drummond's successor on the South Western was Robert Urie, another Scot and one well versed in the requirements of the company's motive power department. He built no more D15s, preferring two-cylinder 4-6-0s of simple and straightforward construction, but, following complaints in November 1914 of heavy fuel consumption by his H15 class, he had the honesty to admit to the Locomotive Committee that on similar duties the Drummond 4-4-0s burnt considerably less coal; details were as follows:

Class	*Type*	*Waterloo–Bournemouth West*	*Average train loads*
		Coal burnt per train mile	
		lb	*tons*
D15	4-4-0	34.83	304
L12	4-4-0	35.12	282
T9	4-4-0	32.94	254
T14	4-6-0	47.64	324
H15	4-6-0	45.07	351

So closed the career of Drummond, one of the greatest Victorian locomotive engineers. Like others in railway service he found it difficult to adapt to the rapidly changing motive power requirements of the 20th century and on occasion found success elusive. Nevertheless, he left the South Western with a well-balanced and able stock of locomotives and in Eastleigh one of the finest and most modern locomotive works in the United Kingdom. This establishment remains active today as a continuing monument to Dugald Drummond, locomotive engineer.

A superheated D15, No 467 outside Eastleigh Works, March 1917.

CHAPTER SIX

THE GREYHOUNDS AT WORK – THE MIDDLE YEARS

Despite the presence of several 4-6-0 classes, the South Western in 1912 remained predominantly a four-coupled line, for most of the express and semi-fast passenger services were still worked by the Drummond 4-4-0s. Since over half were Greyhounds, their main line presence had obviously lost little in importance with the passage of time and the introduction of larger and more powerful locomotives. True, some of the hardest duties had passed to the D15s and 4-6-0s, but there remained numerous other services capable of taxing them to the full, while should one of the larger locomotives fail, then a Greyhound was always willing and able to act as a substitute. Seldom on such occasions could the performance be faulted.

From the turn of the century all main line services had been rescheduled, not only to offer faster timings, but also greater convenience to passengers wishing to change trains at Basingstoke, Eastleigh, Salisbury, Southampton and Exeter. Consequently, it was more important than ever that expresses ran to time and at several Locomotive Committee meetings in the spring and summer of 1912 Drummond was able to report that 97 per cent of all main line passenger trains had arrived to time or not more than two minutes late.

On the Bournemouth line, there were two expresses daily, the 9.08am up and the 4.10pm down, which offered two-hour non-stop journeys while to the West of England the best services were noticeably swifter:

DOWN:

10.50am	Waterloo–Exeter	2.02pm.	Time 3hr 12min
11.00am	Waterloo–Exeter	2–15pm.	Time 3hr 15min
11.10am	Waterloo–Exeter	2.24pm.	Time 3hr 14min
3.30pm	Waterloo–Exeter	6.45pm.	Time 3hr 15min

All stopped at Salisbury only, where five minutes were allowed for engine changing, an operation most crews completed with time to spare.

UP:

10.17am	Exeter–Waterloo	1.47pm.	Time 3hr 30min
12.00pm	Exeter–Waterloo	3.15pm	Time 3hr 15min
12.55pm	Exeter–Waterloo	4.28pm.	Time 3hr 33min
2.10pm	Exeter–Waterloo	6.00pm	Time 3hr 50min

Only the 12.00pm ran non-stop to Salisbury where five minutes were allotted for the change-over operations, the other expresses also calling at Sidmouth Junction, Yeovil Junction, etc to pick up.

Milk traffic from the West Country to London had grown rapidly since the introduction of vacuum-braked vans in 1904 and by 1912 offered the company a handsome profit. Frequently these vans were attached to semi-fast services, but the majority were formed into trains and worked to passenger schedules to ensure that the milk reached Waterloo as rapidly and as fresh as possible. Adams Jubilee 0-4-2s had charge for some years, but by 1912 the T9s had relieved them. One of these turns took a Nine Elms engine from Waterloo at 10.12pm with the empties to Templecombe, Milborne Port, Sherborne and Yeovil, the return being with the semi-fast 6.08am to London, while another brought an Exmouth Junction member of the class up to Waterloo with the 4.10pm vans from Templecombe. The return in this instance was on the 3am passenger and empty milk vans to Yeovil Junction and a stopper to Exeter. With so many small-wheeled mixed traffic 4-4-0s available they might have been expected to receive such tasks, but this was not so on the South Western. Indeed, this use of passenger locomotives persisted until the cessation of steam locomotion in 1967.

The Greyhounds may have had to share the Bournemouth and West of England expresses with other classes, but on the Portsmouth line they excelled themselves and enjoyed an almost complete monopoly of the express and semi-fast services. Here, too, there had been accelerations and with the introduction of new and heavier stock the 74¾ miles proved an imposing task even for such able 4-4-0s. The best down express, the 12.45pm from Waterloo, with brief stops at Guildford, Fratton and Portsmouth Town, was allowed 1hr 55min, while the 2.45pm up, with an additional stop at Vauxhall, took 2hr 3min. On Sundays, when suburban traffic in and around London was light, it was common for the Metropolis to be reached in under two hours, but during the week delays from Wimbledon inwards made exact time-keeping difficult. Consequently, most drivers aimed at reaching Woking with a minute or two in hand and, if possible, at maintaining this insurance until approaching Clapham Junction. In the summer of 1913 one of the morning trains was delegated to the T14 4-6-0s, but they raised objections from the civil engineer as well as proving rather cumbersome and lacking in acceleration, and were quickly

	Engine No.	456	284	113	
	Class	G14	T9	T9	
	Type	4-6-0	4-4-0	4-4-0	
	Load	210 tons	242 tons	238 tons	
	Weather	Fine, light breeze	Showery, high westerly wind	Northerly wind, moderate	
Distance	*Location*	*Actual time min/sec*	*Actual time min/sec*	*Actual time min/sec*	*Schedule*
0.0	Salisbury	00.00	00.00	00.00	0.00
2.5	Wilton	5.18	5.42	5.40	
8.2	Dinton	11.32	12.21	12.30	
12.5	Tisbury	15.58	17.00	17.45	
17.5	Semley	21.52	22.42	24.00	
21.6	Gillingham	25.43	26.21	27.45	
28.4	Templecombe	31.59	32.16	33.40	
	Milborne Port	34.57	35.09	36.45	
34.5	Sherborne	38.22	38.25	40.10	
39.1	Yeovil Junction	42.41	42.13	43.50	43.00
41.3	Sutton Bingham	44.56	44.28	46.00	
47.9	Crewkerne	51.41	51.29	52.40	
	Milepost 133	53.56	53.56	—	
	Hewish Gates Box	—	—	56.35	
55.9	Chard Junction	60.20	60.31	61.30	
61.0	Axminster	64.37	64.47	65.30	67.00
64.3	Seaton Junction	67.33	67.45	68.10	
67.0	Milepost 150½	71.26	72.11	71.55	
69.0	Milepost 152½	75.02	77.15	76.10	
70.0	Milepost 153½	76.42	79.29	78.15	
71.2	Honiton	78.01	80.57	79.45	
75.8	Sidmouth Junction	82.05	84.46	83.30	
79.5	Whimple	85.22	87.57	86.25	
83.2	Broad Clyst	—	—	89.15	
84.9	Pinhoe	90.05	92.17	90.45	
86.9	Exmouth Junction	92.08	94.08	92.35	
88.1	Exeter	93.56	95.59	94.40	96.00

Left: T9 4-4-0 No 300 heads a down West of England corridor express through Earlsfield in 1913. The fourth vehicle is one of the clerestory-roofed Surrey Warner dining cars.

returned to the Bournemouth expresses for which they were better suited.

Notwithstanding their excellent performance on the Portsmouth expresses, the Greyhounds were probably at their best on the Salisbury–Exeter line where the succession of banks gave drivers ample opportunity to employ their propensity for climbing and fast downhill running to the extreme. With such free-steaming boilers it was possible to attack every bank aggressively, for once past the summit it was no problem marshalling resources in time to meet the next obstacle to their flying progress.

The quality of performance is well illustrated by the runs tabulated on page 51 with the 5.09pm Salisbury–Exeter in June 1911.

Although time was kept, the performance of No 456 with a light train was typical of the Drummond P14 and G14 classes, adequate but colourless with steady hill climbing and laboured running down the banks. On arrival at Exeter the driver told the recorder that the steam pressure seldom exceeded 160lb/sq in and that on several occasions there was slipping at speed.

In contrast, the two 4-4-0s, in particular No 113, did remarkably well and, although at some disadvantage with their heavier loads uphill, showed a clean pair of heels once over the summit. Indeed, No 113 ran wonderfully freely down the banks with speeds of 75 to 87mph, following each other in rapid succession, while the 13¾ miles from Honiton to Pinhoe were covered in 11min at an average speed of 75mph. Probably even more informative was the recorder's reference to the safety valves frequently discharging steam to the atmosphere.

The South Western main line from Waterloo to Basingstoke to the casual observer appears easily graded and not overtaxing on locomotives commencing their journeys with clean fires and other kindred advantages. In fact, it was the very reverse with several awkwardly sited banks and entailed much hard slogging which called for a free-steaming boiler and a well-designed front end. Two runs here, one with a G14 class 4-6-0 and the other with Greyhound No 732, fully justify the suggestion that the latter had little to learn from their successors.

With a heavy train, the G14 was content to maintain schedule and found the extra three minutes to Basingstoke over the best timings very necessary. There was a slight check approaching Esher, but speed reached 61mph at the foot of the long climb to Brookwood where the summit was topped at 48½mph. The run

Engine No		457	732	
Class		G14	T9	
Type		4-6-0	4-4-0	
Load		337 tons	298 tons	
Weather		Moderate, westerly wind, dry	Very strong side wind, heavy rain	
Distance	*Location*	*Actual time min/sec*	*Actual time min/sec*	*Schedule*
0.0	Waterloo	0.00	0.00	0.00
3.9	Clapham Junction	8.00	7.30	8.00
7.3	Wimbledon	12.20	11.50	
12.0	Surbiton	17.50	17.10	
14.4	Esher	20.20 (pw slack)	19.45	
19.1	Weybridge	25.45	24.35	
24.4	Woking	31.30	30.30	31.00
28.0	Brookwood	35.35	34.55	
33.2	Farnborough	41.55	41.35	
40.0	Winchfield	48.45	48.50 (signals)	
47.8	Basingstoke	57.10	57.30	57.00

thence to Basingstoke averaged 56½ to 60mph with the boiler pressure falling to 147lb/sq in.

No 732 with a lighter load, but having to contend with a near gale force wind and heavy rain, gave a much more lively start and gained time to Woking with speeds of 57mph at Surbiton, 46½mph at Brookwood and 57mph at Farnborough. At Winchfield the rain became torrential and with the gale made conditions on the footplate most unpleasant as well as making the sighting of signals difficult. There was a slight check after passing Winchfield, but recovery was rapid and only half a minute was dropped to Basingstoke.

During 1913/14 Dr Worley of Salisbury travelled regularly to Waterloo and, being interested in locomotive performance, kept a journal recording details of his journeys. Not all were timed, while particulars of others were incomplete or abruptly ended when delays occurred, but 63 were sufficiently detailed for the preparation of the following table:

Engine class	T9	D15	L12	G14/P14	T14
Number of runs timed	21	6	7	19	10
Average time (min/sec)	52.47	51.19	54.18	57.02	52.56
Average load (tons gross)	296	320	315	340	335
Average speed (mph)	54.4	55.9	52.8	50.3	54.2
BEST RUN:					
Engine No	712	467	418	453	461
Time (min/sec)	51.49	50.37	52.41	50.09	51.31
Load (tons gross)	280	300	270	330	320
Average speed (mph)	55.3	56.4	54.4	57.2	55.7

An up White Star boat express with the then new steel panelled corridor coaches known unofficially as 'ironclads', passes Earlsfield in July 1919 in the charge of No 282. *[Real Photographs*

These figures fully confirm facts handed down over the years by men who were familiar with the day-to-day running of the Drummond express classes before the first world war. The 4-4-0s, in particular the T9s and D15s, were consistently good with periods of brilliance, whereas the performance of the 4-6-0s varied from mediocre to adequate, except on those rare occasions when all went well on the footplate. Then, like No 453 quoted above, their running surpassed any other Drummond class.

In the up direction the line from Basingstoke to Surbiton usually offered drivers a speedy approach to the Metropolis, although thereafter delays were frequently met from the suburban services. Occasionally the road remained clear right into Waterloo and then the 49min timing from Basingstoke was easily cut by three or four minutes, an illustration of this being the run made by No 773 in September 1912.

Distance	*Location*	*Actual time min/sec*	*Schedule min/sec*
0.0	Basingstoke	0.00	0.00
7.8	Winchfield	6.53	
14.6	Farnborough	12.54	
19.8	Brookwood	17.55	
23.4	Woking	20.54	22.00
28.7	Weybridge	25.15	
33.8	Esher	29.30	
35.8	Surbiton (distant came off as train approached)	31.45	
40.5	Wimbledon	36.20	
43.9	Clapham Junction	39.35	42.00
46.5	Vauxhall (slowing for signals)	42.53	
47.8	Waterloo	45.48	49.00

No 773 was three minutes late passing Basingstoke and the driver evidently made up his mind to reach Waterloo to time. The load was 262 tons, the weather fine and no checks were suffered until approaching Vauxhall, where the signals came off as the driver applied the brakes. It was a good, fast and expertly planned run into Waterloo with the driver taking every opportunity with his free-steaming engine and the clear road.

At the outbreak of hostilities with Germany in August 1914, the Urie mixed traffic 4-6-0s and a proportion of the Drummond G14, P14 and T14 classes were immediately removed from passenger duties and set to work on the many heavy goods and munition trains bound for Southampton Docks. Unlike the Second World War, this port played a major role in the passage of material of all types to the armed forces as well as the embarkation of troops. Consequently, the storage, siding and berthing facilities were hurriedly expanded, while for much of the war the running shed at Eastleigh had a greater allocation of heavy locomotives than any other depot on the system. To reduce servicing time a larger turntable was installed and the triangle at the rear of the yards modified to permit use after dark. Incidentally, F13 class 4-6-0s Nos 330–34 during these years worked very high mileages on the Salisbury–Southampton goods and gave full compensation for their earlier failures in passenger service.

A Bournemouth express headed by T9 No 708 overtakes a suburban electric near Earlsfield June 1922.
[Real Photographs

Fortunately, in 1914 the South Western possessed a surplus of locomotives and with a reduction in civilian traffic was able to cater well for the changed pattern of services. Aldershot and the Salisbury Plain stations became centres of army activity, while Portsmouth and Portland fulfilled similar roles for the Admiralty. Very seldom did a day pass when there were calls for less than 30 specials, while before and during offensive actions on the Western Front the Running Department had to call on every locomotive and carriage the company possessed, as well as cancelling many civilian services. On occasions, however, even this proved insufficient and stock had to be borrowed from other railways. It was then that Nos 337/8, together with other Westinghouse-equipped locomotives, were in particular demand for working coaches off lines employing the compressed air brake. This was especially so for horse box traffic, since the vast majority of these trains originated on the Great Eastern or London Brighton & South Coast Railways. Indeed, for several weeks before the great Somme offensive the South Western was also forced to borrow five Wainwright C class 0-6-0s with dual braking from the South Eastern & Chatham Railway, although in fairness to the South Western it must be stated that its own locomotives for the period of the attack were running as far east as Tonbridge and Paddock Wood. In addition, engines were on loan to the Somerset & Dorset and the Midland & South Western Junction Railways, where the wartime demands on local motive power had similarly outstripped resources.

Later in the war there were regular workings by Drummond 4-4-0s from Aldershot and Salisbury Plain to Tilbury Docks via Clapham Junction, Kew, Cricklewood, Kentish Town and the Tottenham & Hampstead line. The South Western also provided and equipped 11 10-coach hospital trains which met ships transporting the wounded from France at Southampton and conveyed them via Basingstoke or Salisbury for onward transit by the Great Western. It was always remarkable to note a Greyhound at work on one of these trains which handed over to a massive Churchward 4-6-0. Many were the quips offered by crews of the latter, but the Drummonds appeared capable of taking away the returning trains with equal ease and lack of slipping.

Commencing in August 1916 50 of the Adams 395 class six-coupled goods were sold to the War Department for service in Mesopotamia, Palestine and Salonika. After repair at Eastleigh Works they were towed away in batches of three for shipment from Barry, Avonmouth, Swansea, Liverpool and London docks. Most travelled via Salisbury, where the Great Western took over, but No 719 was noted hauling Nos 0168, 512/4 north of the Thames on 14 January 1918, bound for the Royal Albert Docks. The loss of so many 0-6-0s naturally left the South Western short of goods locomotives and for the first time it became possible to see Drummond express 4-4-0s regularly working main line and pick-up goods services. Ten 0-6-0s were borrowed from the Midland and the Great Northern railways, and a number of aged and derelict Beattie engines were hurriedly refurbished and returned to traffic, but did little to relieve the situation.

In early 1917 a tank warfare school was established on heath land adjoining the Bournemouth–Weymouth line at Wool and thereafter trains of flat wagons carrying armoured vehicles and coaches for their crews were a common sight. Generally embarkation was at Southampton Docks, the trains being worked there by T9s, often in tandem. One of these trains, No 705, on 16 October 1917, overran signals approaching Bournemouth Central station and collided at 25mph with a line of empty coaches standing on the up through road. Damage was extensive and the station was closed for some hours, but by good fortune no-one was seriously injured. At the subsequent inquiry it was stated that the vacuum pipes of the three coaches next to the engine had not been attached to No 705's vacuum hose and were thus unbraked. Unaware of this, the driver supposed he had their braking power as well as the engine's and consequently, approaching Central Station, with the added hazard of wet rails, was unable to stop when he found the signals at danger. A few weeks later, on 23 November 1917, a similar train headed by T9 No 702 came to grief at Brockenhurst when one of the armoured vehicles broke loose from its fastenings and fouled a passing goods train. Once again casualties were slight.

At Bournemouth in January 1919 the top link consisted of D15s Nos 467/8/9/70 and Greyhounds Nos 722/3/73, these seven 4-4-0s sharing the Waterloo services which, if less tightly timed

No 715 stands at Nine Elms shed in May 1920. It has fluted coupling rods, boiler barrel clack boxes and the smokebox door adorned with a star.
[H. C. Casserley

than pre-war, were nevertheless more heavily loaded and had additional stops. Similarly, Nine Elms was employing Nos 281, 303, 704/29 in the same link as D15s, while the class almost had complete monopoly of the Waterloo–Portsmouth and Salisbury–Exeter semi-fasts. The work expected of these moderately sized and not yet superheated 4-4-0s is well exemplified by a fine of £3 given to Driver Wallis of Exmouth Junction in December 1918 for losing 4½min with a troop special from Honiton to Andover Junction loaded to 403 tons. It has often been stated that the Stanier Black Fives won the second world war for the LMS, and with equal justification the same could be said of the Greyhounds and the South Western during the earlier conflict, for they could be seen all over the system, working every type of train from the heaviest of expresses to the meanest of pick-up goods. Eastleigh for much of 1918 was rostering one for the early morning freight to Weymouth, which stopped to shunt and pick up at every yard en route and spent 16¾hr in so doing. Truly Drummond would have been pleased with their achievements.

At the Armistice in November 1918 the South Western had no fewer than 37 large and powerful locomotives of four types on order from Eastleigh Works at an estimated cost of £300,000:

Type	*Class*	*Engine No*	*Date ordered*	*Delivered*	*Cost*
					£
4-6-0 goods	S15	497–501	10 October 1915	1920	8,406
4-6-0 goods	S15	502–506	27 January 1916	1920	9,567
4-6-0 goods	S15	496, 507–15	29 March 1917	1920/21	10,037
4-6-0 passenger	N15	738–745	27 January 1916	1918/19	7,252
4-8-0T shunting	G16	492–495	10 October 1918	1921	9,536
4-6-2T goods	H16	516–520	10 October 1918	1921/22	9,434

Two N15s had recently been completed and work on the remainder had commenced, but it was impossible to predict when assembly of the others would be possible, for not only were materials in short supply but there was a large backlog of locomotives awaiting general repairs. During hostilities mileages between successive visits to Eastleigh Works were progressively increased with the Urie H15s averaging 184,000 miles. No such figures were possible with the Greyhounds, although in 1918/19 the lowest mileage of those accepted for general overhaul was 71,643, not inconsiderable for such middle-aged Victorian 4-4-0s.

Consequently, apart from the loan of some ROD 2-8-0s for heavy main goods duties, Urie was forced to rely on his own resources and at once instituted a crash programme of general repairs to ensure that as many passenger locomotives as possible were returned to good mechanical order before the summer of 1919. Many Greyhounds required heavy boiler work after years of make do and mend, and to avoid lengthy delays in returning such useful locomotives to traffic, boilers were borrowed from the smaller wheeled L11 class. As a result several of the latter could always be noted around the yards at Eastleigh minus their boilers while few weeks failed to see two or more Greyhounds despatched to traffic. As June 1919 approached, so repainting became a luxury and Nos 113/9, 703/26 spent much of the summer running in shop grey before returning in the autumn for the full passenger livery.

By 1920 the company's stock of locomotives had returned to the excellent mechanical order existing pre-war and with much overdue work completed on the permanent way the speed and frequency of services gradually improved, although not reaching 1914 standards. With the entry into traffic of the 20 large and powerful S15 class 4-6-0s the mixed traffic H15s were reserved for express duty and with the 10 Urie N15s worked all the best services, except over the Bournemouth line where the Drummond D15s remained in charge of many London workings. In the winter months the smaller Drummond 4-4-0s lost much of their main line express work and were mainly employed on semi-fast duties or the cross-country services, such as those between Portsmouth and Salisbury or Southampton and Waterloo via the Alton line. However, summer brought the Greyhounds and L12s back once again to regular express work, especially on Saturdays when shed foremen were thankful to have the former on roll for their popularity, and wide route availability made it possible to entrust them with practically any duty. Superheating from April 1922 made them even more attractive and at Grouping they formed one of the most generally useful classes entering Southern Railway stock.

CHAPTER SEVEN

THE COMING OF SUPERHEATING

In Robert Urie the London & South Western not only gained another exceptionally capable mechanical engineer, but also one fully appreciative of the rapidly changing pattern of railway operation. No longer valid was the use of firebox water tubes, duplex feed pumps, steam driers and feedwater heaters, for all cost more to install and maintain than they saved in hard cash. Accessibility, reliability and simplicity were current requirements which made questionable the provision of inside cylinders, clack boxes tucked away between the frames and tenders having inside bearings and springing. He also realised the company's need of successful six-coupled passenger locomotives and at once set about remedying this deficiency by introducing his two-cylinder H15 class. Later these powerful 4-6-0s were followed by basically similar classes for both heavy goods and express passenger service, while large 4-6-2 and 4-8-0 tanks completed his big engine policy. Urie was a firm exponent of superheating and after initial trials in 1914 it became a standard fitting for all new construction.

The success of any building programme having such an emphasis on the heaviest passenger and goods services depended for success on the presence of a basically sound stock of locomotives to fulfil the many other main line duties. Thanks to Drummond this was the case, for all his express classes, except the earliest 4-6-0s and perhaps the experimental double-singles, were performing well and remained much in evidence on the services to Portsmouth, Southampton Docks, Bournemouth and Exeter. Urie was the first to acknowledge their worth, yet at the same time appreciating that even better performance was possible by the removal of time-expired appliances and the addition of superheaters.

Like many Scotsmen, Urie by nature was cautious. Therefore, although convinced that superheating had much to offer railway service, he approached its general application to the Drummond classes with the utmost prudence and much attention to detail. As a result he restricted its use severely until time and operating experience had proved factual the theoretical advantages of fitting superheaters to older locomotives already giving excellent service. His approach to the problem is readily apparent from the table below.

Surprise might be expressed at the low order of priority granted the Greyhounds, but this was explainable by Urie's desire to improve first the performance of those Drummond classes not regularly attaining their full potential. The later Drummond 4-6-0s and larger 4-4-0s all fell withing this category for, although their performance was sound, their work was seldom relative to their size or coal and water consumption. Under normal conditions a Greyhound skilfully driven and energetically fired could take over an express from one of these larger locomotives and do equally well at about half the cost. The Greyhounds in 1914 were doing very well without the benefits of superheating and, therefore, could be safely left until other less satisfactory classes had been modernised. It was a wise

Class	*Type*	*Date superheating authorised*	*Remarks*
F13	4-6-0	29 May 1919	Cancelled except for No 334
E14	4-6-0	22 April 1914	Cancelled, rebuilt to H15 class
T14	4-6-0	Four only 22 April 1914 Remainder 7 October 1915	All superheated by March 1918
G14, P14	4-6-0	7 October 1915	Only No 449 superheated, remainder cancelled in favour of S11 class 22 November 1917
D15	4-4-0	Four only 22 April 1914 Remainder 7 October 1915	All superheated by September 1917
L12	4-4-0	One only 22 April 1914 Remainder 22 November 1917	All superheated by June 1922
S11	4-4-0	All class 22 November 1917	Substituted for G14 and P14 classes
700	0-6-0	One only 9 October 1919 Ten more 30 June 1921	Remainder by Southern Railway
M7	0-4-4T	One only 22 July 1920 Eight more 25 May 1922	 Cancelled by Southern Railway
T9	4-4-0	Twenty-five 30 May 1921	Remainder by Southern Railway

Above: No 702 stands outside Eastleigh Works in May 1923 after being rebuilt with Urie superheater, extended smokebox, stovepipe chimney and fluted coupling rods.

Below: No 773 at Plymouth Friary in July 1924, showing the tall chimney capuchon, clackboxes repositioned on the boiler barrel and the Urie power classification on the buffer beam valance. *[H. C. Casserley*

policy and one which served Urie and the South Western well.

In a report to the Locomotive Committee in May 1914, Urie stated that he anticipated a saving in coal consumption of from 11 to 16 per cent by the addition of superheaters to the Drummond D15, G14, P14 and T14 classes, but only 6 per cent with the early 4-6-0s. Unfortunately, other statements made on the subject between March 1916 and May 1923 do not explicitly mention the coal consumption details of these classes before and after superheating. He was more concerned with rebuilding costs and amounts of coal saved per engine mile, and

it is from these details that the following table has been compiled:

Class	*Type*	*Cost of superheating*	*Coal saved per engine mile*
		£	*lb*
T14	4-6-0	527	4.9
D15	4-4-0	472	3.4
L12	4-4-0	488	2.7
S11	4-4-0	494	1.8
700	0-6-0	335	7.9
M7	0-4-4T	348	0.9
T9	4-4-0	496	4.7
F13	4-6-0	607	No 334 burnt 2.3lb more coal
P14	4-6-0	581	No 449 burnt 1.6lb more coal

The greatest saving was shown by the 700 class 0-6-0 No 316 when tested on main goods services between Nine Elms Yards and Salisbury in April 1921:

Engine No	*No of journeys*	*Average load*	*Coal burnt per train mile*	*Saving by super-heating*
		tons	*lb*	*lb*
316 (superheated)	11	647	52.3	7.9
688 (saturated)	5	628	60.2	—

When the same two engines were compared shunting the yards at Feltham the difference in coal consumption was minimal, but the significance of this evaded Urie and he later built four superheated 4-8-0 tanks for these duties.

During 1920 Urie and his Eastleigh pattern superheater were the subject of several complaints of patent infringement by the Marine & Locomotive Superheaters Company. Royalty payments totalling £4,980 were demanded on 64 locomotives, this being calculated at £65 each, plus interest charges since superheating. At first, the South Western and Urie refused to accept the charge, but later, after further correspondence and investigation, it was agreed to pay £500 providing no further demands were made and the company could use the superheater when desired without hindrance. This proved acceptable and Urie, after making several minor modifications, was able to sell his rights to the Southern Railway for £1,000 in October 1923.

Superheating the Greyhounds was first given serious consideration in October 1917, but, because of hostilities with Germany, no action was taken until after the armistice. Therefore, during the first world war modifications to the class were restricted to removing the firebox water tubes and repositioning the clack boxes on the sides of the boiler barrel. Attention was also given to the lubrication of the tender axleboxes and an attempt made to reduce the volume of grit finding its way to the bearing surfaces. The boxes and springs of these 4,000 gallon double-bogie tenders were tucked away between the framing and the wheels where they were difficult to see and maintain at the running sheds. Urie heartily disliked the layout and ensured that the 5,000 gallon tenders he provided for his three 4-6-0 classes had these items in full view where any trace of trouble could be readily detected and rectified.

After the 1918 armistice many months were to pass before a semblance of normality returned to the South Western and authorisation could be granted for the superheating of 25 Greyhounds at a cost of £496 each. The drawings were prepared in May 1921 and it was hoped to have the first rebuild, No 314, back in service by the New Year, but delays in obtaining materials prevented this, and it was April 1922 before the erecting shop was finally left. Apart from the superheater, rebuilding included an extended smokebox, stove pipe chimney with tall capuchon and 19in cylinders, while the boiler had been stripped to the barrel and provided with new tubes, tubeplate, inner copper firebox and outer casing. It was to all intents and purposes completely new. The expense and added complication of fitting piston valves was avoided by improving the lubrication of the flat slide valves by the introduction of a four-feed hydrostatic lubricator. The changed dimensions were:

Cylinders	19in × 26in
Heating surfaces:	
Tubes (124 × 1¾in) (21 × 5¼in)	921sq ft
Firebox	142sq ft
Superheater	195sq ft
Total	1,258sq ft
Weight in working order:	
Bogie	17tons 1cwt
Leading coupled wheels	17tons 12cwt
Trailing coupled wheels	16tons 14cwt
Total	51tons 7cwt

Unlike other Drummond classes superheated by Urie, the boiler pitch was not raised, but this had minimal effect on the appearance and No 314 remained an extremely attractive looking 4-4-0. Five others, Nos 300/4/5/11/3, were

Above: Superheated Greyhound No 284 passes Esher with a Weymouth express September 1923.
[H. Gordon Tidey

Below: No 314 of the wide cab T9 series, seen after superheating passing Walton-on-Thames in July 1923 with a Union Castle boat express. *[H. Gordon Tidey*

similarly rebuilt before the end of 1922, leaving the remainder of the order to be completed by the Southern Railway. Typical mileages at superheating were: No 300–687,413; No 304–699,118; No 314–644,967.

The Eastleigh superheater was derived by Urie in 1915 from the well known and widely used Robinson type. It differed mainly by being less complicated and simpler to dismantle, for the top and bottom headers were little more than distribution chambers attached to the lower connecting pieces, and alternately joined to the upper saturated and lower superheater headers. The four-fold element tubes commenced at the saturated header and returned to the superheater header, while the individual tubes passed through the connecting members to be secured by bolts at front and rear. The three vertically arranged elements, therefore, each formed a complete set which was quite independent of any other and, with ease, could be removed for access or maintenance without interfering with the remaining elements. In regular service it gave complete satisfaction and was considered by Eastleigh Works as being cheaper to maintain than the Maunsell pattern superheater which superseded it after Grouping.

Shortly after its return to traffic, No 314 was transferred to Bournemouth and at once took its share of the more lightly loaded London expresses. Later it was joined there by Nos 300/5/11/3, when they practically monopolised the Bournemouth–Weymouth services. Most London trains changed engines at Bournemouth Central with the front portion of down expresses being taken forward to Dorchester and Weymouth by locally shedded 4-4-0s, while M7s or T1s hauled the main portion round to the West station. In the up direction the coaches from Weymouth arrived at the Central first and, after the engine was uncoupled, were hurriedly drawn back by the station pilot to a siding parallel to the engine shed to await the main train. This came round from the West station with little delay behind the locomotive destined to haul the combined train forward to Waterloo, the latter having worked round tender first to the West station about 30min earlier. The Weymouth coaches were

Below: At work in the West Country, No 729 accelerates away from Okehampton with the through Portsmouth–Plymouth train on 23 September 1923.
[Ken Nunn/Locomotive Club of Great Britain

attached as quickly as possible and the express sent on its way. If time was to be kept, it was essential for the Weymouth train to arrive on schedule and the Jubilee or T1 0-4-4 tank acting as pilot to perform its task with the minimum of fuss and delay. Seldom could the Greyhounds be faulted for late arrivals.

A number of trial runs were made with No 314 during the autumn of 1922 and the following is a selection of the performances given:

Regulator opening	*Percentage cut-off*	*Speed*	*Boiler pressure*	*Steam chest pressure*	*IHP*
		mph	*lb/sq in*	*lb/sq in*	
Half	70	10	175	160	407
Half	60	18	175	161	762
Three-quarters	40	37	175	164	998
Full	35	49	175	169	844
Full	35	53	172	166	1,045
Full	30	73	170	164	848
Full	30	81	175	166	1,068
Full	30	62	175	166	762

Coal consumption per train mile on Bournemouth line expresses varied from 28.64lb with 168 tons to 30.83 with a much heavier load of 276 tons. Best Welsh coal, picked over and loaded on the tender by hand, was employed throughout the trials.

The class had always been well liked by the men and over the years had created an enviable reputation for speed and reliability. They were equally well thought of at the running sheds for they were easy to work on and required the minimum of maintenance. Consequently, much was anticipated from superheating and expectations were amply justified, for not only did speed potential remain but the boiler became a prodigious provider of steam. Relative to its size, it was the best in the South Western and over the years must have become the friend of many an inexperienced and tiring fireman.

Robert Urie and the Motive Power Department thus gained some of the most able and willing moderately-dimensioned express locomotives in the country, a fact that R. E. L. Maunsell, the Chief Mechanical Engineer of the newly formed Southern Railway, quickly appreciated, for he authorised the superheating of the entire class: 1922, Nos 300/4/5/11/3/4; 1923, Nos 119, 282/4, 301/2/3/10/36/8, 702/4/9/21/2/4/9/73 (No 773 was renumbered 733 in December 1924 to make way for the North British Locomotive Company built King Arthur class 4-6-0 No 773 *Sir Lavaine*); 1924, Nos 121, 287, 307, 705/7/14/5/26; 1925, Nos 113/6, 283, 312/37, 706/13/27; 1926, Nos 122, 285/6/8, 703/19/25/8; 1927, Nos 114/5/7/20, 280/9, 708/11/6/7/30/1/2; 1928, Nos 118, 281, 712/8/23; and 1929, No 710. After superheating the Dübs and first Nine Elms series had the following working order weights:

Bogie	16tons 4cwt	17tons 2cwt
Leading coupled wheels	18tons 10cwt	18tons 7cwt
Trailing coupled wheels	17tons 2cwt	16tons 9cwt
Total	51tons 16cwt	51tons 18cwt

After December 1924 Maunsell superheaters were substituted for the Eastleigh pattern, with a heating surface of 213sq ft and could be detected by a pair of snifting valves on the smokebox top. Those superheated earlier were similarly modified when next in works for general repair. Three new boilers were built at Eastleigh in 1923 and fitted to Nos 119/21, 287, but all the other rebuilds received renovated boilers. Two more new boilers were built in 1928 and supplied to Nos 312/38; like the 1923 batch they retained the dome top lock-up safety valves and other Drummond features, although they could be recognised by the more rounded dome covers and Urie firedoors.

The tall stove pipe chimney carried a prominent capuchon, but this was later shortened and eventually omitted altogether, although Nos 119 and 721 ended their days so equipped. Other changes concerned the coupling rods and sandboxes. When new, like the S11s and L12s, the class was fitted with flat coupling rods, but the D15s and 4-6-0s received a fluted pattern and it was this variety which came into use from 1922. Most engines received them on superheating, but there were exceptions, including Nos 284, 311 and 729. Similarly the prominent splasher-mounted sandboxes of the Dübs and first Nine Elms series remained *in situ* for some years before being repositioned between the frames.

CHAPTER EIGHT

GROUPING – THE EARLY STAGES

At the grouping of railways in 1923, the London & South Western was merged with the South Eastern & Chatham, London Brighton & South Coast and several smaller companies to form the Southern Railway. Of the locomotive works at Eastleigh, Ashford and Brighton, those at Eastleigh were undoubtedly the most spacious, modern and best equipped. Therefore, although the new Chief Mechanical Engineer, R. E. L. Maunsell, was from the South Eastern & Chatham Railway, this establishment was called upon to play an increasingly important role in the maintenance and construction of the new company's steam stock. On numerous occasions during the next decade Maunsell must have been eternally grateful for Drummond's foresight and expertise when setting out and equipping the erecting shop and other buildings there.

Altogether 912 London & South Western locomotives entered Southern Railway stock, this total, of course, including the 66 Greyhounds. For a time all repaints were in the full Urie livery, but from the end of October 1923 supplies of Southern green became available and it was applied to all passenger locomotives passing through works. The lining was in yellow, while the company's title was inscribed across the tender or tank sides above the engine number, which was prefixed by the letter E (for Eastleigh)' to distinguish Western Section stock from locomotives originating on the Central (B), Eastern (A) and Isle of Wight (W) Sections. These prefixes were retained until mid 1931 when Maunsell belatedly introduced a more logical numbering system in which Western Section locomotives, except for the duplicate stock, retained their pre-grouping numbers, but 1000 and 2000 respectively was added to the numbers of ex South Eastern & Chatham and London Brighton & South Coast locomotives. For this reason no account is taken here of the E prefix when mentioning Western Section stock between 1923 and 1931.

Commencing with Nos 113 and 715 in December 1923, 15 Greyhounds, Nos 113/21, 338, 705/6/7/8/11/4/5/6/9/26/31/2, received this livery before the Chairman decided it was too insipid and ordered Maunsell to find a more impressive substitute. At the time, January 1925, No 314 was in Eastleigh Works for general repair and before being returned to traffic was painted an attractive sage green with black and white lining. It was inspected by the directors at Waterloo on 14 February and, being approved, became the standard livery until after Maunsell's retirement.

No 282 in Southern Railway livery, May 1925, with Maunsell superheater, snifting valves and smokebox door secured by additional clips. *[Real Photographs*

Superheating proceeded apace, although on account of the number of locomotives involved, it was July 1929 before the last, No 710, returned to traffic rebuilt. Because of this lengthy period many ran for some years in Southern colours, while remaining saturated. Very seldom, however, were they rostered for main line duties, for they were incapable of offering the same performance as the superheated examples. Often they were relegated to odd mixed traffic duties or piloting heavy expresses, while Bournemouth regularly employed Nos 118, 281 and 710/23 on the Swanage branch.

In early 1924 Maunsell ordered a detailed evaluation of the Southern's motive power when it became evident that a large surplus of medium-powered passenger locomotives would arise during the following years. Many could be advantageously discarded when next despatched to works for major overhaul, but it was imperative to discover those classes which were best retained for secondary passenger duties before instructions for wholesale withdrawals were issued. Consequently, in April and May 1924 a series of trials with classes B1, B2X (ex LB&SCR), T9 (ex LSWR) and F1 (ex SE&CR) were held on passenger services between Brighton, Hastings and Ashford. Each engine was prepared by its home shed, driven by crews familiar with the class and fired with the type and quality of coal normally employed. No details of these trials were published at the time, but a summary was found at Ashford Works when the drawing office was being reorganised in 1957:

Class	*Engine No*	*Time lost during week*	*Coal burnt per train/mile*	*Maintenance cost*	*Remarks*
		min	*lb*	*units*	
B1	172	13	37.9	133	Injector fitted Gladstone 0-4-2, boiler priming badly
B2X	206	27	39.9	137	Top feed to boiler, priming trouble, one injector failed
B2X	208	21	42.1	124	Side feed to boiler, poor steaming, much clinker
F1	204	7	31.4	92	Poor quality fuel, free steaming
T9	314	0	26.8	100	Superheated, best Welsh coal, safety valves set to 180 lb/sq in

All trains were made up to two three-coach ex SE&CR sets and a bogie van, of which only the leading three coaches were available to the public. The maintenance cost was standardised at 100 units for the T9 and the others graded according to their higher or lower charges for the period.

No 314 was always working easily and probably lost more steam via the safety valves than was gainfully employed until the crew accurately gauged the moderate demands of the 120 to 140 ton trains. The success of the saturated rebuilt Stirling F1 came as a surprise to all concerned, except the Ashford contingent, while the two B2Xs gobbled up alarming quantities of coal with but little visible account except dense clouds of smoke and lineside fires. The Gladstone was too old for serious consideration.

As a result it was decided to withdraw all the ex LB&SCR Gladstones and B2Xs, and to replace them on the Central Section by Stirling B1 and F1 4-4-0s, while their loss to the Eastern Section was made good by the transfer of 10 superheated Greyhounds to Battersea. Consequently, in January 1925, No 707 appeared on several Victoria–Margate semi-fasts, but was quickly laid aside when the overall length proved too great for some of the Eastern Section turntables. On further consideration it was decided to equip those transferred with the shorter 3,500 gallon six-wheeled tenders off the 700 class goods and also to restrict the choice to those having the full width cabs. Nos 310/2/4 reached Battersea in February 1925, where they were followed during the next six weeks by Nos 300/1/4/7/11/3/36. At this period the Kent Coast services from Victoria were desperately short of suitable motive power, for they were subject to such stringent restrictions that the heaviest permitted classes were the rebuilt D1 and E1 4-4-0s. The Greyhounds, therefore, proved a most welcome addition to Eastern Section stock and at once appeared on the business and other expresses to Margate and Dover via Chatham and Faversham as well as occasionally on the lighter continental expresses. They proved very popular with Battersea crews who expressed surprise at their moderate coal and water consumption.

In the days of steam Sole Street bank always

No 727 in August 1925 with its sandboxes removed from the splashers and repositioned between frames.
[Real Photographs

proved an excellent test of a locomotive, for the long climb from Rochester Bridge had to be commenced at reduced speed, usually about 30mph, so much of the initial impetus was lost by the time Cuxton Road box was passed. The average speed thence over the four miles to Sole Street station presented a good comparison of the effort sustained by various classes. The following table analyses 105 runs made in 1928/38:

Class	T9	L12	D1	E1	L	L1
Number of runs	24	5	21	17	17	11
Average speed (mph)	32.6	31.8	31.4	32.0	31.2	28.9
Average load (tons)	234	293	225	230	250	320
BEST RUN:						
Time (min/sec)	7.01	6.48	7.08	6.27	7.13	7.08
Average speed (mph)	34.2	34.8	33.6	37.2	33.3	33.6
Load (tons)	287	314	280	260	285	350

A large proportion of these recordings were made after the stringent weight restrictions had been removed following the completion of major bridge strengthening and permanent way works, but the general pattern of performance remained much as it was when the Greyhounds were first transferred to Battersea in 1925.

Drummond L12s Nos 416/7/9/24/30/1 were sent to Dover and Nos 421/2/5/33 to Bricklayers Arms in the summer of 1925 to replace ex SE&CR L class 4-4-0s on the smartly timed Charing Cross–Dover expresses. They proved a great success, but after the new L1 class 4-4-0s Nos A753–59, A782–89 entered traffic in the following year Nos 424/33 were transferred to Battersea and the remainder to Brighton and Fratton. Towards the end of 1928 Nos 417/9/21 returned to Battersea and worked many of the secondary services before being despatched to Redhill in July 1929, while Nos 424/33 were sent to Fratton. For some years the class made few appearances on the Eastern Section, but, following the mid Sussex electrification in July 1938, Nos 416/9/22/30/1/3 reappeared at Battersea and at once took over a number of secondary express and semi-fast duties to Ramsgate over both the Chatham and Sevenoaks routes. It was mid 1940 before all had returned to the Western Section.

Other interesting Greyhound transfers in early Southern Railway days included Nos 281/2, 303, 704/26/9, with six-wheeled tenders, to Brighton in mid 1928 for use on the through Bournemouth train and the Portsmouth services. Odd appearances were also made on the London semi-fasts, while on at least two occasions visits were made

Above: A familiar sight for some years after the grouping; a pair of Greyhounds, Nos 337 and 704, pass Raynes Park with a heavy down express.

Below: A West of England express descends Hewish bank headed by No 284 in August 1928.
[*H. C. Casserley*

Right: A saturated Greyhound in Southern livery, No 285 at Salisbury, July 1925. [*H. C. Casserley*

to Tunbridge Wells West. Their stay, however, was not prolonged and by October 1928 Nos 281/2 were working from Battersea on Eastern Section duties, where they were joined by Nos 303 and 726 in the following year. No 729 was returned to the Western Section at Salisbury, while No 704 was transferred to Battersea Park.

For some years after grouping the two Victoria running sheds, Battersea (Longhedge) and Battersea Park, kept themselves very much apart, with the former covering Eastern and the latter Central Section duties. However, from 1928 onwards King Arthurs had daily turns over the Central and this was soon followed by regular use of L12s and T9s ,though at first this appears to have been mainly at weekends, particularly in the then numerous National Sunday League excursions to the coast resorts. By 1930 they were to be seen in some numbers on such workings as Victoria–Hastings via Polegate, also to Eastbourne and Bognor Regis, and had also taken over the 9.45am Victoria to Brighton (Sunday Third Class Belle), a 69min run, including stops at Clapham Junction and Croydon, a far from easy task with the eight fully-laden Pullmans.

At long last in 1932 came the removal of the Kent Coast restrictions which enabled a wider use to be made of the Greyhounds and from January 1933 they replaced U class 2-6-0s on the 10.45am down Eastbourne Sunday Pullman. On the same date this express was accelerated to give an 80min journey, then the fastest ever and a timing only bettered by one minute under electric power. Today the fastest is 83min and this is seldom kept. Although the winter load was light, the 10.45am remained a Greyhound duty throughout the summer when a top loading of eight 40-ton cars proved an exacting task, yet one which was invariably accomplished with a few seconds in hand. Moreover, in the summer of 1933 this working with the same fast timing became daily, but formed of two Pullmans and five or more Marsh high roof coaches. More often than not a Greyhound had charge, although occasionally a King Arthur made an appearance.

From this time, too, the class took an increasing part in the mid Sussex line workings from Victoria to Bognor Regis and Portsmouth, and were diagrammed for duties such as the 9.5am Victoria–Portsmouth Harbour and the 2.55pm back. They had been, of course, for many years a familiar sight on the mid Sussex line, but previously as Western Section residents of Fratton or Nine Elms sheds. As this line's

On the Central Section in July 1930, No 304 heads the Sunday Third Class Brighton Sunday Pullman near Hassocks. *[Real Photographs*

restrictions became tighter so the Greyhounds appeared to increase their hold on the workings until the last steam summer of 1937, when even the Maunsell 2-6-0s were barred, and they really ran riot. On Sundays Littlehampton and Bognor sheds were teeming with them, though not all from Battersea.

Towards the end of 1932 Nos 313/36 were transferred to Brighton and employed almost exclusively along the coast line to Portsmouth, except in the summer months when they regularly headed the Brighton–Ashford on the Wednesday and Sunday excursions to the Kent resorts.At this period Brighton was employing L12s Nos 417/21/5 on the through services to Salisbury, although it is probable that Nos 313/36 also made occasional appearances. These two were still at Brighton in 1935, but in June 1936 No 336 was transferred to Battersea while No 313 was joined by Nos 303/4 until the autumn when all three went into store at Eastbourne. The following spring saw them again back at Brighton where they remained until December 1937 when all 16 small tender Greyhounds, Nos 281/2, 300/1/3/4/7/10/1/2/3/4/36, 704/26/9, were concentrated at Battersea. Over the years few foreign locomotives have proved so acceptable for such a lengthy period of time.

Another interesting stretch of line for testing hill climbing ability was that between Tonbridge and Tunbridge Wells Central on the Hastings branch of the former South Eastern Railway. Although only a distance of 4.9 miles the line climbs at 1 in 53 immediately after curving sharply away from the London–Dover main line steepens to 1 in 47 and then varies between 1 in 72 and 1 in 300 until High Brooms – three-and-a-half miles – where running becomes considerably easier. This was, of course, for many years the hunting ground of the Schools, but other classes were also regular performers, while the Greyhounds appeared with specials from Denmark Hill to Hastings on most Whit and August Bank Holiday Mondays during the 1930s as well as with van trains at Christmas. The following table is an analysis of 90 runs on this steep section and gives a comparison between classes E1, D1, L1, L, Schools, I3, N1 and T9.

Class	E1 & D1	L1	L	Schools	I3	N1	T9
Number of runs	7	14	13	39	10	3	4
Average time (min/sec)	12.14	12.38	12.18	11.06	11.47	11.46	11.51
Average speed (mph)	24.0	23.3	23.9	26.5	24.9	25.6	24.8
Average load (tons)	198	304	287	344	186	318	218
BEST PERFORMANCE:							
Class	E1	L1	L	Schools	I3	N1	T9
Engine No	1504	1788	1770	901	2081	1878	301
Time (min/sec)	11.38	9.55	10.54	10.08	10.20	11.06	10.29
Average speed (mph)	25.3	29.7	26.9	29.1	28.4	26.5	28.0
Load (tons)	283	245	340	360	208	320	234

The L1 class 4-4-0s were not renowned for hill climbing, therefore the exceptionally smart timing recorded by No 1788 is worthy of note for it surpassed most performances given by the more powerful Schools. The Greyhounds with comparatively light trains did reasonably well and on average were better than the more extensively modernised D1s and E1s. The only really heavy train taken over the Hastings line by a Greyhound, No 336 and 340 tons, was unfortunately piloted from Tonbridge by D No 1057. Nevertheless, the time of 10min 13sec for the 4.9 mile climb was most presentable.

Of equal interest, although for a different reason, was the 26.6 mile line between Ashford and Tonbridge, for being straight and practically level, it gave crews every opportunity to show how speedy their charges were. Before the arrival of the Bulleid Pacifics, the Schools held pride of place, though on occasions other classes, including the Greyhounds, ran them closely. The following table is compiled from 92 such runs:

Class	T9	L12	D1	L1	Schools
Number of runs	8	19	9	32	24
Average speed (mph)	64.6	65.2	63.8	65.4	66.3
Average load (tons)	275	305	290	320	345
BEST RUN:					
Time (min/sec)	22.27	22.31	23.27	22.56	22.09
Maximum speed (mph)	81	80.5	79	76.5	85
Load (tons)	190	280	225	340	380

Returning now to the Western Section and the majority of the Greyhounds, it was quite obvious from lineside observation at Basingstoke, Bournemouth and Exeter that the new Maunsell classes had not usurped all the main line duties. On summer Saturdays Greyhounds could still be noted at the head of heavy expresses, while good use was made of their wide route availability and excellent power ratio to work many of the through trains to the Great Western via Salisbury or Reading. During 1925/30 one of these duties regularly took one of the Bournemouth engines as far north as Birmingham Snow Hill with loads varying between eight and eleven bogie coaches. On most Saturdays only one Greyhound was required, but on 28 July 1928 No 288 had charge of the main 10-coach train while No 118 followed 10min later with seven Great Western carriages. The shed at Bournemouth always carefully prepared engines chosen for these services the previous Friday and early on the Saturday morning piled as much coal as possible on the tenders. When leaving the yards to take up the train at the Central station, the shed foreman often travelled on the footplate to see the crew off on their journey. At this period, and for some years after, there was a daily duty from Salisbury which took Nos 285, 713/27/9 through to Bristol, while right down to the second world war excursions from Western Section stations to Weston-super-Mare gave the Bristol Channel coast regular sightings of the class. They also proved most useful for the Waterloo–Weymouth holiday services routed via Ringwood and West Moors to relieve congestion at Bournemouth Central. A run timed as far as Worting Junction behind No 705 in July 1931 gave the following lively performance with 10 well-laden coaches:

Distance	Location	Time min/sec	Speeds mph
0.0	Waterloo	0.00	
1.3	Vauxhall	3.29	
3.9	Clapham Junction	7.08	41
7.3	Wimbledon	11.14	57
12.0	Surbiton	16.06	60
19.1	Weybridge	22.41	65
24.4	Woking	27.34	
28.0	Brookwood	31.17	54
33.2	Farnborough	37.08	
36.5	Fleet	40.23	62
42.2	Hook	46.06	57
47.8	Basingstoke	51.42	53
50.3	Worting Junction	54.48	

Until the arrival of the Maunsell three-cylinder U1 class 2-6-0s, the Portsmouth line via Guildford also made demands with Nos 287, 337/8 and 712 regularly assisting the larger D15s. Occasionally in the summer months, when loads warranted it, they hunted in pairs over this far from easy route. A further source of activity was offered by the Ocean Liner specials to and from Southampton Docks, while yet another was with the Channel Islands boat trains. Possibly the heaviest express headed by a Drummond 4-4-0 since South Western days was the down St Malo of 23 December 1928, which consisted of no fewer than 10 Maunsell corridors and seven ex LSWR bogie coaches, weighing about 500 tons. No 113 made a slow start and dropped 7½min to Worting Junction, but thereafter ran so rapidly down through Winchester and Eastleigh that the arrival in the Docks was only 2¾min down.

In the up direction Ocean Liner expresses provided equally fine running with No 708 in April 1929 taking 11 corridors up to Waterloo in 87¼min from Northam Junction:

608
OKEHAMPTON

SOUTHERN
287

SOUTHERN
705

Top left: The North Coast portion of the Atlantic Coast Express enters Okehampton behind No 709 on 22 July 1936. *F. M. Gayes*

Centre left: On the shops road at Eastleight in May 1936, No 287 with intermediate chimney and short capuchon. *Photomatic*

Bottom left: Nine Elms, April 1937; No 705 carries the final pattern stove pipe chimney. *G. Alliez*

Distance	*Location*	*Time min/sec*	*Speeds mph*
0.0	Northam Junction	0.00	
4.5	Eastleigh	6.59	48
13.6	Winchester Junction	19.04	44
21.9	Litchfield Box	29.14	43
27.8	Worting Junction	36.37	68
30.3	Basingstoke	38.44	73
38.4	Winchfield	45.38	64
44.9	Farnborough	51.42	
50.1	Brookwood	56.47	
53.7	Woking	59.52	73
59.0	Weybridge	64.20	63
64.8	Hampton Court Junction	69.40	
70.8	Wimbledon	76.18	52
74.2	Clapham Junction	80.34	
78.1	Waterloo	87.14	

When compared with the daily work of the King Arthur or Lord Nelson 4-6-0s the performance was not exceptionally enterprising, but for a 30-year-old Victorian 4-4-0, not at all bad.

By the early 1930s the introduction of the Schools class 4-4-0s and the U and U1 2-6-0s had removed many of the Greyhounds' traditional main line duties, especially from Bournemouth, where 2-6-0s had charge of the through services, and this trend towards more mundane duties is shown by the allocation of June 1932: Dorchester Nos 286/8, 705/30/1; Eastleigh Nos 114/20, 302/5, 708/24; Exmouth Junction Nos 117, 283/4, 703/10/1/7/9/23/32; Feltham No 118; Fratton Nos 115/9, 287, 337/8, 702/7/12; Plymouth Nos 116, 709/14/5/8/22/33; Guildford Nos 706/25; Nine Elms Nos 122, 280/5/9; Salisbury Nos 121, 713/27/9; Yeovil Nos 113, 716/21/8; Central Section No 704; Eastern Section Nos 281/2, 300/1/3/4/7/10/1/2/3/4/36, 726.

At Guildford Nos 706/25 had a regular daily duty over the Reading–Redhill line, where otherwise most of the passenger services were in the hands of ex South Eastern & Chatham 4-4-0s or Maunsell 2-6-0s. As this line abounded in steep gradients and difficult starts four-coupled locomotives demanded skilful driving and firing if schedules were to be kept. Another interesting Guildford duty concerned the through Margate–Bournemouth West coaches. In the up direction they were coupled to the rear of the Birkenhead train as far as Guildford; there they were removed, augmented by three more coaches and several vans, and taken on by one of the T9s. Until electrification of the Waterloo–Portsmouth services the route was via Havant and Netley, but thereafter it was by way of Aldershot, Alton and Eastleigh. The climb up the steep bank out of Alton with a heavy train was always most exhilarating and vocal, but there was little doubt who was master.

The Greyhounds transferred to the Eastern Section in 1925 had the tall and rather ungainly chimney capuchons lowered to reduce the overall height to suit the more restrictive SE&CR loading gauge. Similar modification was made to those despatched at a later date to the Central Section, although in their case it was not essential, while the remainder of the class when in need of new chimneys received this pattern. However, commencing with No. 731 in June 1932, a plain stove pipe became standard, but, as was usual on the Southern Railway, changes came gradually and several engines, including Nos 119 and 721, went to the scrap yard still carrying short capuchons. Such chimneys probably suited the class best, the final pattern being rather too stark. No 119 had always been considered a good engine and because of this was often rostered for royal or other important special duties; therefore, when undergoing general repairs in mid 1935 it was given VIP treatment to make it more suitable for such work. This consisted of a beautifully executed green livery with the engine and tender wheels lined out, black shaded gilt lettering and numerals and highly burnished metalwork. Chromium plating was used for the snifting valve caps and many of the footplate fittings, including the lower part of the regulator, gauge casings, cocks and valve wheels. In addition, an organ pipe whistle was fitted, while plaques with the royal coat of arms were provided for attachment, when necessary, to the leading splashers. On returning to traffic in July 1935 it was loaned to Bournemouth for a few days to work the Swanage branch, but was then despatched to Nine Elms for the special

At work on the Eastern Section, T9 No 281 nears Teynham with a Ramsgate excursion in August 1933. *[Real Photographs*

conveying King George V to Portsmouth Harbour for the Silver Jubilee Naval Review.

By the mid 1930s many of the four-coupled passenger tender locomotives taken into Southern Railway stock at grouping had quite outlived their usefulness and had been withdrawn from service or were working out their final mileages on light duties. All the ex LB&SCR Gladstones and B2Xs had gone, while inroads were being made into the Drummond C8s and the ex SE&CR F1s and B1s, but fortunately the Greyhounds did not come into this category, for they remained in great demand. New boilers were required, but no funds were available and resort once again was made to the fitting of new fireboxes, tube plates and tubes to the original Drummond barrels. Over the years the mileages worked between successive general repairs had progressively increased and, if seldom bettering those of the Maunsell classes, were nevertheless by 1936 most respectable. Details for the 1923 to 1936 period were:

	Intermediate repair		*General repair*	
Dates	*Miles*	*Months*	*Miles*	*Months*
1923/26	29,685	16.2	53,641	27.3
1933/36	37,014	19.6	71,016	31.4

These are average figures for the class and in 1923/26 all 66 engines were concerned, but for the 1933/36 period only 47 members were involved, the other 19 engines not appearing twice at Eastleigh Works for general repairs during these years. In 1933/36 intermediate repairs averaged £239 per engine and tender while general overhauls cost £646.

The T9 repair mileages compared most favourably with those run by the various Eastern Section 4-4-0s in 1933/36, as will be noted from the following table:

	Intermediate repair		*General repair*	
Class	*Miles*	*Months*	*Miles*	*Months*
L1	29,665	18	76,445	31
L	24,885	16	73,340	26
D1	28,670	18	69,865	29
E1	24,130	17	65,470	27
D & E	21,225	19	71,890	34

Despite the cramped site and dated equipment at Ashford Works, the standard of workmanship was as high as that found at Eastleigh, while the costs in 1936 averaged $6\frac{1}{2}$ per cent less. Eastleigh's advantage lay in the shorter time taken giving both general and intermediate repairs.

Victoria on August Bank Holiday Saturday 1936 saw much of the class, for the following expresses were in the hands of T9s: No 301 9.10am to Dover Marine; No 704 11.25am to Bognor Regis; No 336 11.42am to Portsmouth Harbour; No 281 12.35pm to Margate, No 300 relief 1.10pm down Continental; No 314 2.25pm to Bognor Regis; and No 726 relief 4.10pm to Portsmouth Harbour. Others, including Nos 304 and 311, were working the Cannon Street–Sheerness trains in place of E class 4-4-0s required on other holiday services, while Nos 307 and 313 reached Hastings via Tonbridge on excursions from the London suburban stations and No 310 was engaged on the Tonbridge–Redhill stoppers.

The last down steam passenger train over the mid Sussex line, the 7.20pm Victoria–Portsmouth and Southsea on 2 July 1938 was worked by No 115 of Fratton shed, while I3 class 4-4-2 tank No 2029 hauled the last up train. The engines had been specially cleaned for their tasks and given noisy send-offs, and to prove that steam had only been superseded, not outclassed, both

Above: No 119 in the paint shop at Eastleigh on 30 June 1935 splendidly painted specially for royal train working. *[H. C. Casserley*

Below: On special duty, No 716 deputising for 119 heads the royal train near Peasmarsh Junction on its way to Portsmouth for the Coronation Naval Review in 1937. *[D. E. H. Box*

gave early arrivals to the many enthusiasts sampling steam on this route for the last time.

Other interesting turns around this period included through excursions from Brighton to Frys of Somerdale, these being formed of eight corridor coaches and three Pullman cars and headed by Nos 303/4/13, while Battersea found Nos 282 and 336 equally useful for the Victoria–Wye race specials. On the Western Section the use of Southampton Water for the Imperial Airways flying boat services made it necessary to provide special expresses, first from Victoria and later from Waterloo. Loads were light and seldom exceeded a Pullman car, one first class corridor coach and a bogie van, but the schedules were fast and offered crews every opportunity to show their paces. Various classes were involved, including T9s Nos 281, 301/7/10, 704/5/6. Therefore, as the Maunsell era drew to a close, the class remained fully active and still capable of working all but the heaviest of expresses. Already they had seen three locomotive superintendents/chief mechanical engineers come and go, and they were about to meet yet another.

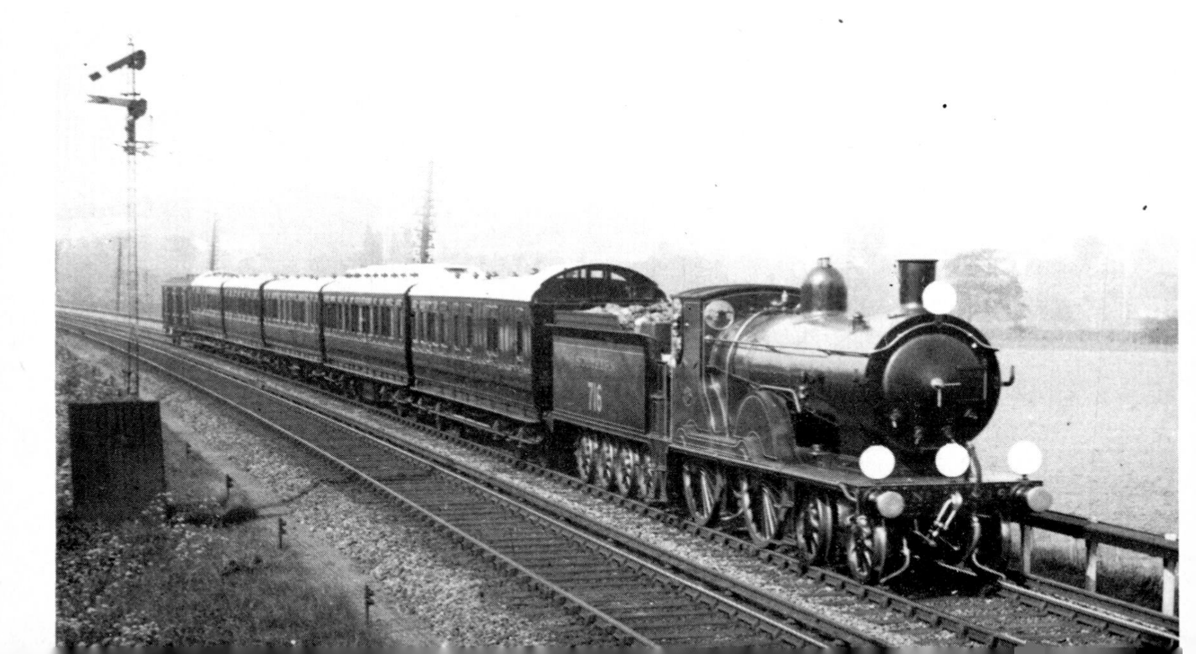

CHAPTER NINE

GROUPING – BULLEID AND THE WAR YEARS

Unlike the LMS, the Southern Railway from grouping until October 1937 experienced no major change of leadership and consequently enjoyed a continual and balanced expansion of services and amenities. The emphasis under the benevolent, if bureaucratic, rule of Sir Herbert Walker was with suburban and main line electrification, and this led the company from undistinguished pre-grouping performance to become the most successful British railway capable of paying regular dividends of 5 per cent. With the private motorist and long-distance coach operator not as yet a serious menace, he proved that railways could operate profitably and at the same time remain positively attractive to the clientele.

This achievement came at a period when office workers in London were being slowly and remorselessly edged away from the centre by congestion and a rise in property values in many traditionally middle class districts. Status could only be maintained by migration to the Home Counties. Under Sir Herbert's guidance and zeal the Southern Railway led an all-embracing onslaught on the countryside of Kent, Sussex, Surrey and Hampshire by creating a network of electrified commuter services. Once these became operational and were experienced by potential home buyers, thousands of new houses were constructed and sold, connecting the farms, villages and market towns into the vast subtopian sprawl of today.

The trade depression of the early 1930s did not affect the southern counties of England so severely as it did the remainder of the country and, although money was lost by the Southern's steam services, receipts from the electrified lines increased steadily, for city workers much appreciated their cleanliness, punctuality, frequency and speed.

Not content with revitalising the inner suburban services, Sir Herbert cast the company's sights further afield and electrified to Brighton and Worthing in 1933, Sevenoaks, Eastbourne and Hastings in 1935, and Portsmouth in 1937. At once these lines also recorded sizeable receipt increases and gave rise to visions of complete electrification with the steam locomotive being gradually phased out of traffic. Funds, therefore, were sparingly allotted for new steam construction with many elderly locomotives having to be repaired and kept at work when otherwise they would have been scrapped and replaced. This policy, of course, favoured the Greyhounds, for with their excellent reputation and economy they escaped all threats of withdrawal whenever the spread of electrification necessitated the judicious pruning of steam stock. All consequently were in existence and gainfully employed on secondary services throughout the three sections when ill health forced Maunsell to tender his resignation in October 1937.

The same month found G. S. Szlumper succeeding Sir Herbert Walker as General Manager, while on 1 November 1937 O. V. Bulleid came from the LNER as the new Chief Mechanical Engineer. For some years Maunsell had been prepared to accept the secondary role of steam, but not so his successor, who appreciated that a decade or more must pass before it could be entirely discarded and in the meantime many important Southern main line services would have to rely on steam locomotives for their motive power. Consequently, a fresh and more inspiring image was essential if the best was to be gained from existing locomotives, while the General Manager and directors were persuaded to allot greater funds for new construction. After careful consideration Bulleid decided this was best achieved by changing the livery and between April and June 1938 he investigated various hues of green and a variety of lining and lettering styles on N15 class No 749 *Iseult*. These experiments culminated in the following month with the appearance of Schools Nos 925/6/7/8/9/30/2 and several sets of coaches painted malachite green for service on the Bournemouth Limited and other expresses over that line.

Although most attractive, Bulleid apparently was not entirely satisfied by this light green because in November 1938 Eastleigh Works applied olive green to Lord Nelsons Nos 855/6/61/3, and for some months both colours appeared indiscriminately on the larger express passenger classes. Time and the elements, however, proved that the olive green was poor wearing and prone to fading; therefore, the light

or malachite green was standardised until wartime restrictions in April 1942 caused the substitution of plain black.

The first small passenger locomotive to receive the Bulleid livery was No 119, the royal engine. On 10 June 1938 it left Eastleigh Works painted olive green with black and white lining, cabside numerals and the tender lettered Southern. An interesting and practical innovation was the painting of the tender raves green to allow the lettering to be lined up with the cab numerals. Previous Bulleid repaints had the lettering and numerals at different levels, which spoiled the symmetry and suggested a paint shop error. It will be recalled that Maunsell-liveried tender locomotives carried small oval cast numberplates on the cabsides but had their numerals inscribed on the tenders below the company's title. This led to difficulties if for some reason or other it became desirable to transfer tenders from one locomotive to another, and no doubt was the reason for the numeral repositioning by Bulleid. Experience on the LNER must have suggested the change for some years earlier that company had experienced the same problem.

No other Greyhounds were painted olive green, for it was decided to use up stocks of Maunsell sage green on the less important passenger locomotives and to reserve the new colours for such classes as the Lord Nelsons, Schools and King Arthurs. Over the next two years, therefore, the T9s re-entered traffic after general repairs in the following liveries:

June to August 1939: Maunsell green, black and yellow lining, tender numerals – Nos 116, 285, 311, 722.

October 1939: Maunsell green, no lining, tender numerals – Nos 713/4/25

November 1939 to October 1940: and again *January to March 1941:* Maunsell green, no lining, cabside numerals, Bulleid lettering – Nos 113/4/7/20/1/2, 284/7, 305/7/36, 702/3/7/8/9/11/7/9/23/8/30/1

October 1940 to January 1941: malachite green, no lining, cabside numerals and Bulleid lettering – Nos 115, 302/10, 704/16/22

March 1941 onwards: plain black, cabside numerals and Bulleid lettering. No 721 was the first to suffer this indignity and left Eastleigh Works on 19 March 1941.

The outbreak of hostilities with Germany in September 1939 led immediately to a major change of policy, for once again steam had become the most important source of motive power. No further escalation of electric services could be contemplated for some years and steam locomotives scheduled for withdrawal were granted an extended lease of life. Many new goods and passenger locomotives were to be built at Ashford, Eastleigh and Brighton Works for the company's services, while Stanier 8F 2-8-0s were constructed for use on the other major lines.

As far as the Greyhounds were concerned it was business as usual, although a number of transfers were necessary to meet the changed working pattern of wartime. The first of these occurred in the West Country where the three-cylinder U1 class 2-6-0s, in use by Exmouth

No 115 stands at Southampton Central with the Portsmouth–Cardiff through train in August 1938.
[R. F. Roberts

Junction since mid 1937, were despatched to the Redhill–Reading services and their places filled by Nos 282, 300/1 from Battersea and Nos 721/4/5/30/1 from elsewhere on the Western Section. Other transfers from Battersea took Nos 310/2/4 to Salisbury, from where they appeared on the Portsmouth trains and occasionally those to Bournemouth. At Battersea their loss was made good by D1s Nos 1487, 1509, 1741/3/7, which shared many Chatham line semi-fast duties with Nos 281, 303/4/7/11/3/36, 704/26/9, the remaining Eastern Section members of the class. One interesting duty covered the following trains: 6.05am Holborn Viaduct–Ramsgate via Maidstone East and Canterbury West, 11.18am Ramsgate–Tonbridge via Folkestone, station pilot at Tonbridge, 7.10pm Tonbridge–Ashford (rear four coaches off the 6.18pm Cannon Street–Ramsgate), 9.23pm Ashford–Swanley.

On the Western Section, forces leave trains began running from Southampton to Waterloo in mid October 1939 and at first were worked by a variety of locomotives, including King Arthurs, H15s and S15s, but towards the end of the year set trains of eight corridors and two restaurant cars were formed shared by Drummond Paddleboxes and Nos 705/6/7/8/28. These trains were always well loaded and with reasonably smart schedules for wartime were quite a task for such elderly locomotives, although they invariably performed well. Another source of work for Eastleigh engines was the daily ambulance train which conveyed injured BEF personnel from Southampton Docks to Salisbury for onward routing to the Midlands via the Great Western. Two train sets were employed, each consisting of seven converted LMS coaches sandwiched between two Southern bogie vans, the recording numbers being 8 and 11.

By mid 1940 there was no call to retain Greyhounds on the Eastern Section so Nos 281, 303/4/7/11/36 and 727 were transferred away to Nine Elms, No 313 to Eastleigh and Nos 704/26 to Guildford. The last-mentioned joined Nos 714/30 on the Redhill–Reading services and also the daily turn to Southampton Terminus.

The Dunkirk evacuation did not seriously involve the class for most were stationed far away from the Dover main line, but Nos 704/14/26 from Guildford were loaned to Redhill and found their way as far east as Paddock Wood. No 704 spent a day station piloting at Tonbridge and on the following morning worked down to Hastings with empty stock.

Little else of note occured before August Bank Holiday Saturday 1941 when, despite the war, traffic to the West Country was heavy and No 307 was called upon to work a 10-coach relief to the 2.50pm Waterloo–Exeter.

Before the war motive power on the Somerset & Dorset was provided by the LMS and visits by Southern Railway locomotives were largely restricted to the Bournemouth end of the line and to special workings. However, in October 1941 the demands of hostilities necessitated a recall of many LMS locomotives from the line for redistribution to Midland Division depots and the Southern Railway was asked to supply substitutes. Consequently, 10 S11s, six T1s and T9s Nos 303/4/7/12 were hurriedly prepared and despatched to Highbridge for S & D service. Nos 303/7 were no longer required by the end of the year and were returned to the Southern, where they were followed by No 312 in March 1942, but No 304 remained on loan until May 1945. It was usually shedded at Templecombe and employed double-heading 4-6-0s on the heavy through trains or working slows to Bournemouth. In February 1943 it was noted piloting a troop train at Gloucester and later shunted for several days in the yards there, while in the following month it worked a goods into Bristol. A minor mishap occurred on Bath shed during August 1943 which necessitated a visit to Derby Works for attention to the cab sidesheets, running plate and buffer gear.

No 119, the royal engine, had been so well painted before the war that the olive green livery remained in good order until 1944. Stationed at Eastleigh, it was regularly cleaned and when necessary employed on special workings where a clean, green locomotive relieved the wartime gloom. These included a visit by King George VI to Portsmouth Dockyard, General Montgomery to Weymouth and General Eisenhower to Southampton Docks and Poole Harbour. A special night service was run at this period of the war between Waterloo and Weymouth and sleeping accommodation was provided by two LNER first class cars on loan from the Scottish expresses. Greyhounds were invariably rostered for the duty with No 119 making an appearance if anyone of note was travelling.

A through train to the LMS passes Kensington (Addison Road) in July 1939 behind No 729. *[R. F. Roberts*

Other interesting workings around this period included No 310 piloting a Great Western Hall on a 16-coach troop special out of Birmingham Snow Hill on 14 April 1944, and No 714 piloting LNER B12/3 class No 8549 with a 14-vehicle ambulance train from Exeter to Clapham Junction on 19 August 1944. Equally unusual was the use of No 288 to haul WD 2-8-0s Nos 70855 and 77266 from a siding at Micheldever to Southampton Docks, while No 113 in the following month was supplying steam to ocean-going vessels undergoing repairs in the King George graving dock. Around D day the Eastern Section once more had use of the class when Nos 281, 336 and 708/12 worked troop specials from Redhill to Appledore via Ashford. They had not, however, completely forsaken the section since 1940, for Eastleigh was unable to accept all Western Section locomotives offered for repair and Nos 288, 300, 705/17/8/9/31/3 perforce had to travel to Ashford for attention.

All 66 engines survived hostilities, although many urgently required heavy repairs and 19 boilers were scheduled for firebox renewals when next in works. Some high mileages had been run between successive general repairs, although the 142,483 amassed by No 702 of Yeovil was exceptional rather than the rule. In September 1945 Nos 336 and 337 were equipped with Flaman speed recorders, these being mounted outside the cab with a suitable aperture provided for viewing the dial. Drive was by means of a vertical shaft from the crankpin of the trailing coupled wheels. The reason for these fittings was to facilitate the running of tests at controlled speeds over various lengths of experimental track laid between Woking and Basingstoke, near Andover Junction, between Wool and Dorchester and near Milborne Port. Later No 337 was engaged in braking tests with new stock between Worting Junction and Eastleigh. At the completion of these tests the speed recorders were removed from No 336 in September 1946 and No 337 in May 1947.

Black remained the standard livery, except for No 119, which left Eastleigh Works in May 1946 painted malachite green with black and white lining, crimson coupling rods and burnished piping for service on royal and other VIP specials. A loudaphone telephone gave communication from the cab to the train staff. The short chimney capuchon remained, but the pre-war chromium plated fittings had either been removed or painted over. One of its early duties occurred on 28 November 1946, when a train of two first class saloons and two new Southern sleeping cars conveyed the directors on a tour of inspection at Southampton and Eastleigh. The party spent the night on the Bishops Waltham branch, with No 702 providing steam heating, and on the next day departed behind No 119 for Dover via the coast road. A second repainting was received in May 1948, when a deep-toned hooter was fitted and the snifting valves removed. The latter had become standard practice in September 1946 with their removal from No 336.

Before the war the quality of fuel provided on the Southern was probably higher than that found on the other major companies, but by 1945 the size and quality of locomotive coal had reached abysmal levels, while the quantity available barely kept abreast of demand. It was not unknown for smaller depots to be entirely without coal and to have to commandeer supplies from wagons destined for local coal merchants. To alleviate the position the

No 114 painted plain black and burning oil fuel stands at Eastleigh on 26 April 1948. [D. L. Bradley

Government authorised the conversion of locomotives belonging to all four main line companies to oil firing, the Southern's quota being:

Class	Scheduled for conversion	Actually converted
T9 (Greyhounds)	15	13
L11	15	8
D15	10	1
N15	10	5
H15	6	0
West Country	20	2
N & U	34	3
Terrier	0	1
	110	33

Conversion of the Greyhounds commenced in January 1947:

Engine No	Date	Electric lighting fitted
113	20 September 1947	15 November 1947
114	10 September 1947	28 February 1948
115	30 August 1947	23 December 1947
118	30 August 1947	26 February 1948
121	30 August 1947	24 January 1948
280	15 September 1947	1 November 1947
286	12 September 1947	8 December 1947
303	20 September 1947	9 February 1948
305	18 January 1947	28 February 1948
314	13 September 1947	22 November 1947
713	2 September 1947	25 October 1947
722	15 September 1947	17 January 1948
731	1 September 1947	31 January 1948
732	Cancelled 8 December 1947	
733	Cancelled 8 December 1947	

All the tenders were of the 4,000 gallon double bogie variety, Nos 303/14 exchanging their small 3,500 gallon tenders for the larger type from S11s Nos 395/7. Welded oil tanks with a capacity of 1,600 gallons were dropped into the coal space and secured there by bolts through the bottom plating. A Bulleid influence was found in the steps on the rear of the tank and a shorter pair at the back of the tender, these being constructed of welded tubing and similar to those fitted to modern Southern locomotives. At a later date Stone's turbo-generators were bolted to the left-hand running plate alongside the smokebox and provided electricity for the route indicator lights and footplate illumination. Like the other Southern oil-burning conversions the Mexican trough system was employed, although originally it had been intended to use the Laidlaw-Drew type on No 314. Instead this equipment was transferred to Brighton Works and in February 1948 saw service on West Country No 21C136.

To enable the best use possible to be made of the oil-burning locomotives refuelling plants with a total capacity of 250,000 gallons were established at Fratton, Eastleigh and Exmouth Junction, while smaller depots for topping-up purposes were set up at Salisbury, Bournemouth, Basingstoke and Nine Elms. The latter could be transferred overnight if required for the main constituents were a rail tanker-wagon, steps, hand pump and hose piping. In addition, D tanks Nos 2244/84 were modified for pumping oil and as Service Stock 700S and 701S were variously employed at Fratton, Eastleigh, Exmouth Junction and Nine Elms. Surely no greater ignominy befell Stroudley locomotives?

No 305, the first conversion, re-entered traffic from Eastleigh Works on 18 January 1947 and for a time was restricted to local passenger and goods duties, but in early February was regularly

Oil burner No 731 pilots D15 No 471 in May 1948. The electric generator is sited on the running plate and powered lights for night-time route indications.
[W. Gilburt

rostered for the 7.46am Eastleigh–Bournemouth Central and 11.48am ex Bournemouth West. As both trains were normally lightly loaded extra coaches were added to offer worthwhile tasks, latterly the weight being 300 tons. No trouble was met keeping time, while a surplus of steam was dissipated in the atmosphere. Appearances were also made on the heavily-loaded through Bristol train, while on 28 June 1947 it piloted Bulleid Pacific No 21C150 from Salisbury to Southampton on the Plymouth–Brighton. At Southampton the train was split with No 305 taking on the Portsmouth portion and the West Country the section for Brighton. Later, when all 13 oil-burners were in service, they were normally employed on local passenger trains in the Portsmouth–Eastleigh–Salisbury area, although occasional sallies were made to Alton on goods, to Basingstoke with vans, and to Salisbury and Bournemouth with stoppers.

Unfortunately, no sooner had the Southern's conversion scheme got fully under way than problems of supply and finance cast doubts on the wisdom of changing from coal to oil burning. By May 1948 oil supplies were severely restricted and the scope of activities gradually reduced until October 1948 when all 13 T9 oil-burners were laid aside in store to await reconversion to coal firing. This, however, never occurred and, after lying derelict for some years, they were condemned by British Railways in April and May 1951, an unlucky fate, for many others not enjoying the same fuel modernisation remained active until 1957/61.

The allocation in October 1947 was as follows: Basingstoke Nos 307, 706/8; Bournemouth Nos 719/28; Eastleigh Nos 120/1, 286, 302/5/13/36, 705/7/13/32; Exmouth Junction Nos 282/3, 301, 723/4/5/30/1/2/3; Fratton Nos 113/4/5/8, 280/7, 303/4/14/38; Guildford Nos 311, 704/26; Nine Elms Nos 119, 718; Plymouth Nos 116, 289, 711; Salisbury Nos 117/22, 285/8, 312, 709/15/21/7/9; Wadebridge Nos 703/17; Yeovil Nos 310, 702/10/2/4/6; and Dorchester Nos 281/4, 300. All except Nos 113/4/5/8/21, 280/6, 303/5/14, 713/22/31 were actively engaged, with No 119 of Nine Elms often appearing on special duties. On 16 April 1947 No 718 had charge of the relief 12.50pm Waterloo–Exeter and with seven corridors and a bogie van reached Salisbury 2½min early. In the West of England whenever the 10am Plymouth–Brighton through train exceeded the loading of a West Country Pacific it was the practice to employ two T9s as far as Exeter, while several of the Exeter–Salisbury slows daily were rostered for the class. At the other end of the scale Eastleigh often employed Nos 120, 302/13/36, 705/7 on mixed traffic and pick-up goods duties, while Basingstoke used Nos 307, 706/8 for station pilot and a daily semi-fast to Waterloo.

CHAPTER TEN

NATIONALISATION AND FINALE

The Transport Act which received Royal Assent in August 1947 was a truly formidable document of 128 sections and 15 schedules, although there was no doubt as to its intention. This was the creation of the first British Transport Commission with the express duty of providing the country with an efficient, economical, adequate and integrated system of public inland transport and port facilities for passengers and freight. The Act also provided for the establishment of public authorities to be known as Executives and, by agreement with the Minister of Transport in the Labour Government, five of these bodies were created, of which the one designated the Railway Executive most concerns us here, since under its guidance the four major British railways and a number of minor companies were divided into six groups to be known as the London Midland, Western, Eastern, North Eastern, Scottish and Southern Regions. The last-mentioned in general with minor additions embraced the Southern Railway, although at a later date boundary changes, after toing and froing, eventually saw the loss of the West Country lines to the Western Region.

Consequently, on 1 January 1948, all 66 Greyhounds entered British Railways stock and in course of time, except for Nos 113/4/6/8, 280, 303/5/14, 713/22/3/31, had their Southern Railway numbers increased by 30000. For a brief period in early 1948, before instructions to this end were received, a limited number of engines left works carrying an S prefix. Only two of the class were involved:

Engine No	*Works*	*'S' Prefix added*	*To 30000 series*	*BR number*
S282	Eastleigh	14/2/1948	1/12/1951	30282
S285	Eastleigh	12/2/1948	31/12/1950	30285

Both were painted unlined black with Bulleid style lettering and numerals, the tenders being lettered British Railways in full.

The first renumbered into the 30000 series was No 30718, which left Eastleigh Works on 22 April 1948, the livery following that of Nos S282/5, except for the change of numeration. Some members of the class receiving general repairs were similarly treated while others not rating such major attention were renumbered but remained with tenders lettered Southern. An exception was the royal engine, No 30119, which was repainted malachite green in May 1948. Numerals continued to appear on the front buffer beams, but with No 30715 in September 1948 they were replaced by LMS type smokebox door numberplates. The tender lettering was of interest, for on No 30119 it was hand painted whereas on other engines transfers were used where the letters could be obtained from the word 'Southern' and hand painted where not. This was difficult to detect except when viewed from certain angles in bright sunlight.

The next change came in December 1948 when No 30729 was painted glossy black with red, yellow and grey lining. The numerals were Gill Sans in yellow while the tender panelling was unlettered pending delivery of the BR lion and wheel totem transfers. From early April 1949 off-white replaced both the yellow of the lining and the numerals. Also of interest was the continued use of the LSWR power classification letters introduced by Robert Urie in March 1916 and perpetuated by the Southern Railway on Western Section locomotives, including the King Arthurs, Schools and Lord Nelsons (see Appendix). Letters were painted on the platform valance immediately to the rear of the buffer beam, unless there was insufficient space, when the sandboxes or splashers were used. In British Railways livery the letter was repositioned below the cabside numerals on engines painted at Eastleigh Works, but invariably omitted from those belonging to the Western Section repainted at Ashford or Brighton Works. This remained standard practice until May 1954 when Eastleigh, and later the other two establishments, commenced applying the October 1953 British Railways (LMS type) power classification above the cabside numerals. In course of time the running sheds also gave assistance with the consequence that engines could be noted carrying both old and new systems. The Greyhounds were classified 3P, the same as classes S11, L12, D15 and Eastern Section 4-4-0s of E1, D1, L and L1 classes.

Somewhat earlier in January 1949 British Railways had introduced a classification system

Top: No 30726 at Eastleigh in April 1949, resplendent in British Railways lined black with plain tender and the Urie power classification below the cab numerals.
[D. L. Bradley

Above: No 30721 at Nine Elms March 1952 with snifting valves removed, but retaining the intermediate chimney and small capuchon.
[B. C. Bending

Left: The only malachite green post-war Greyhound, No 30119, the pre-war royal engine, at Eastleigh in August 1952. *[D. L. Bradley*

Bottom left: No 300 in August 1950 still retaining the six-wheeled tender fitted 25 years earlier for service on the Eastern Section.
[D. L. Bradley

for official use under which the Greyhounds were 2P, but this was not carried by locomotives and had little practical value except when preparing duty rosters or working timetables.

To gain greater efficiency and higher daily mileages, a more intensive use of locomotives was gradually introduced and this made it convenient to know at a glance to which running shed a locomotive was allocated, for it could then be returned home without loss of time. It would also make the unofficial borrowing then prevalent simpler to detect, a factor Eastleigh became aware of in mid 1949 when ELGH was painted LNER fashion on the buffer beams of its larger locomotives. This was only a temporary measure for in August 1950 LMS pattern shed plates were attached to the lower arcs of the smokebox doors. When first applied many plates were unpainted and quickly became illegible through rust, but after a visit to works the figures and letters were picked out in white.

Green undoubtedly suited the class best, although the lined black BR livery when freshly applied or well cleaned gave a reasonably attractive appearance. Southern Region locomotives were usually better cleaned than those of the other regions, with some running sheds, including Eastleigh, Salisbury and Exmouth Junction, taking excellent care of even the humblest classes. Bournemouth frequently neglected its express locomotives, yet for some reason, regularly cleaned its 4-4-0s and 0-4-4 tanks.

Once again the summer of 1948 found the Eastern Section short of passenger locomotives and, as in earlier years, this was overcome by the transfer of Nos 281, 301/4/11/2, 704/26/9 to Battersea for use on the Chatham line semi-fasts. However, on Saturdays they were at once upgraded to full main line status and played an important role working the many Kent Coast services. A brief period of viewing the traffic at Newington on 31 July 1948 found No 301 heading the 11.25am Victoria–Ramsgate, while in the up direction four others appeared in rapid succession on Victoria-bound trains, No 704 with the 1.48pm Dumpton Park, No 729 2.05pm Dumpton Park, No 726 3.15pm Ramsgate and No 304 3.25pm Margate. In all cases the load was three ex SE&CR non-corridor three-coach sets, no great weight, but that day King Arthurs, Schools and Maunsell 2-6-0s were working trains of similar formation. During the summer several of these expatriates were timed up Sole Street bank, a summary of these recordings over the four miles from Cuxton box to Sole Street station being:

Engine No	281	304	311	704	726	729
Date	24/7	17/7	31/7	15/8	17/7	15/8
Time (min/sec)	7.11	8.00	7.14	7.19	7.34	7.01
Average speed (mph)	33.4	30.0	33.2	32.8	31.5	34.2
Load (tons)	225	275	245	290	245	285

Considering the neglect of wartime and the poor quality coal, the times were most reasonable, especially that of No 729 which had a tender full of slack and blasted its way up the bank setting fire to all combustible items.

During the 1948/49 winter Nos 281, 301, 726/9 were stored at Fratton and Nos 304/11/2, 704 at Battersea, but all were back in traffic the following year, although No 282 went to the Eastern Section in exchange for No 704 which remained at Fratton. Their services, however, were not in great demand and much time was spent out of use or substituting for ex SE&CR 4-4-0s under repair or undergoing boiler washouts. Nos 281 and 301 were transferred to Guildford in July 1949 while later the others were similarly despatched to Western Section sheds.

On the withdrawal of the Drummond Paddleboxes the summer of 1950 proved a truly vintage one for the Greyhounds, for they were in great demand for main line service as the following examples illustrate: 8 July, No 30302 10.38am Waterloo–Swanage; 15 July, No 30312 12.20pm Bournemouth Central–Waterloo; 22 July, No 30712 Oxford–Bournemouth through train; 29 July, No 30336 2.20pm Waterloo–Bournemouth; 4 August, No 30302 3.5pm Bournemouth West–Waterloo; 11 August, No 30300 up evening combined Lymington Pier and Southampton Docks special; 12 August, No 30312 1.5pm Waterloo–West of England; 9 September, No 30712 11.39am Waterloo–Lymington and the 3.40pm return working. Never again were they to play such an important main line role, but in passing they certainly left their mark, for the running was of the highest order, so much so in fact that it was difficult at times to appreciate their age and size, especially with other more modern and powerful classes failing dismally during the difficult post-war years.

Unfortunately, 1951 saw the withdrawal of the stored and now derelict oil-burners Nos 113/4, 30115, 118, 30121, 280, 30286, 303/5/14, 713/22/31, as well as Nos 116, 30122, 30281, 30704/14/6, while Nos 30119, 30302/7/11/2, 30703/25/33 went in the following year. Luckily there was then a lull with only Nos 30282/3, 30304/36, 30708/28/30 going before the end of 1957. The frames from No 722, dismantled in April 1951, were stored at Eastleigh Works until December 1954, when they were set up in the erecting shop and married to the cylinders, wheels and other parts of No 30732, the resulting locomotive taking the latter's number. Other interesting happenings at this period included the transfer of 700 class 0-6-0 No 30346's six-wheeled tender to No 30707 in July 1955 and the departure of No 30721 from shops in November 1955 still carrying a chimney with a short capuchon. A very minor feature, admittedly, but one which added much to the engine's appearance.

The RCTS 25th Anniversary Special of 28 June 1953, from Waterloo to Exeter and back to Paddington, with the inclusion of the Lyme Regis branch, gave D15 No 30464, T9 No 30711 and Western Region Star No 4056 *Princess Margaret* every opportunity to demonstrate their prowess. The two Drummonds accepted the challenge, but for various reasons the Star took no less than 4¾hr to reach Paddington.

No 30464 made a slow start to Clapham Junction, but thereafter gave of its best with the running beyond Basingstoke being particularly good. The net time for the 83.8 miles to Salisbury was 90min, one less than the schedule. Here the 245-ton seven-coach train was taken over promptly by No 30711 and on the wonderful route thence to Exeter, Driver Goodver of Exmouth Junction shed treated the participants to all the best that his 40 years' experience of this road and his willing, sure-footed and free-steaming 4-4-0 were capable of producing. The start was marred by engineering works at Dinton, but thereafter the speed rose rapidly to give 78½mph through Gillingham, 78mph before Templecombe and 86mph at Sherborne, while beyond Chard Junction mile after mile was covered at 75mph. The result was that, including the slack at Dinton, the 61 miles from Salisbury to Axminster were covered in 67min 40sec start to stop, some 4¼min under schedule.

Distance miles	*Location*	*Schedule min/sec*	*Actual min/sec*	*Speed mph*
0.0	Salisbury	0.00	0.00	
2.5	Wilton		6.55	63
8.2	Dinton		13.24	60
			pws	22½
12.5	Tisbury		20.35	45
17.5	Semley		27.15	43 (min)
21.6	Gillingham		30.57	78½
23.9	Milepost 107½		32.53	59¾ (min)
28.4	Templecombe		36.40	78
29.9	Milepost 113½		38.27	49 (min)
30.8	Milborne Port		39.26	83½
34.5	Sherborne		42.30	86
39.1	Yeovil Junction	44.00	46.02	75
41.4	Sutton Bingham		48.05	58
42.7	Milepost 126¼		49.41	50½ (min)
47.9	Crewkerne		54.26	66
49.7	Milepost 133¼		57.03	41 (min)
55.9	Chard Junction		62.36	75
61.0	Axminster	72.00	67.40	

Net time after allowance for checks: 64.00min
Gain on schedule: 8.00min

At Axminster No 30711 enjoyed a well-deserved rest while Terrier No 32662 and Adams 4-4-2 tank No 30583 made several journeys over the Lyme Regis line with the specially strengthened branch train. At the conclusion of the last journey No 30711 was smartly away for Exeter, and again the running was excellent with a fine burst of speed down through Whimple and Broad Clyst, giving a maximum of 83mph. After a brief stop at Exeter Central the descent to St David's was made and the train handed over to Star No 4056 *Princess Margaret*.

Distance miles	*Location*	*Schedule min/sec*	*Actual min/sec*	*Speed mph*
0.0	Axminster	0.00	0.00	
3.2	Seaton Junction		6.10	48 (max)
8.8	Honiton Tunnel West end		18.30	22½/26
10.2	Honiton		20.08	80
14.8	Sidmouth Junction		23.55	62/71
18.5	Whimple		27.05	83
22.2	Broad Clyst		29.50	80
24.1	Pinhoe		31.20	65
			signals	
27.0	Exeter Central	37.00	38.20	

Net time after allowance for checks: 35.30min
Gain on schedule: 1.30min

No 30711 was an Exmouth Junction engine but, nevertheless, its day's work was far from over, for it was sent off shed again at 10.15pm to pilot S15 No 30829 to Salisbury with a ballast special from Meldon Quarry.

The class remained fully occupied during 1954 with only No 30282 of Eastleigh shed being withdrawn. At Nine Elms Nos 30718/9 spent much of their time in charge of the Waterloo–Reading van services, while during the summer Eastleigh regularly rostered Nos 30283/7/9, 30310 for the Saturdays only 10.35am Lymington Pier–Waterloo, a 10-coach train. The booked return was with empties for Southampton Docks, but frequently this was cancelled in favour of the 4pm military special to Marchwood. Nos 30705/24 at Basingstoke were strategically positioned to offer assistance or replacement to

Above: The crew of No 30726 watch the photographer as they leave Fordingbridge with the 10.45am Bournemouth West–Salisbury in July 1953 [*S. C. Nash*

ailing locomotives of both up and down expresses; an instance, on 14 August 1954 saw No 30724 taking over the Torrington portion of the up Atlantic Coast express. The same engine on 8 September 1954 had a joyous non-stop trip from Portsmouth Harbour to Waterloo via the direct line when it was specially cleaned and prepared for the special conveying Sir Brian Robertson and other BTC officials. The train consisted of only two coaches, one being the Southern inspection saloon DS291, but the running was excellent with the 100min schedule cut by 4½min. No 30337 of Guildford was a frequent visitor to the Reading–Redhill line, but it was a stranger, No 30719, which on 26 November 1954 had the unusual duty of working a 450 ton train of ballast hoppers from Redhill to Woking. The task was successfully achieved by rushing the banks, a habit undoubtedly perfected by many years of working over the switch-back West of England main line. The allocation in January 1955 was: Nine Elms Nos 30718/9; Guildford No 30337; Basingstoke Nos 30705/24;

Below: The typical South Western scene for more than 50 years, a T9 4-4-0 and LSWR non-corridor lavatory set, used so widely on cross country and main line stopping services. The 6.40pm Andover Junction–Eastleigh passes Stockbridge headed by No 30284 June 1955. [*E. W. Fry*

Fratton Nos 30726/9/30/2; Eastleigh Nos 30117/20, 30283/4/5/7/8/9, 30300/10; Bournemouth Nos 30707/28; Exmouth Junction Nos 30708/9/10/1/2/5/7/27; Salisbury Nos 30301/4/13, 30702/21; and Yeovil No 30706. In the West Country the class still performed regularly over the Plymouth and Padstow lines, being a pleasant change from the Bulleid Pacifics and Maunsell 2-6-0s. One, on occasions, also worked the Exmouth branch goods.

From time to time the class made brief appearances in films and on television, but in February 1957 at Baynards on the rural Horsham–Guildford line No 30310 and M7 No 30026 became fully-fledged stars during the taking of scenes for 'The Railway Children' by the BBC Television Film Unit. Both locomotives had evidence of British Railways ownership painted out and were temporarily renumbered 10 and 26. Great care was taken to give authenticity to scenes involving the locomotives and trains and, when viewed on television, the standard of production was exceptionally high with the Greyhound in particular fulfilling its role exactly.

The lion and wheel BR emblem of 1949 had few pretensions to artistic intent, but nevertheless held sway from 1949 until March 1957 when a more attractive pattern was substituted. This consisted of a demi-lion rampant (the British lion) holding between its paws a silver locomotive wheel, the lion being issuant from an heraldic crown of gold on which were arranged a rose (for England), a thistle (for Scotland), a leek (for Wales) and an oak leaf (for all Great Britain). The whole was enclosed in a gold circle and flanked by the words British Railways in serif gold lettering. No 30726 on 16 May 1957 was the first Greyhound to make the change and was followed by Nos 30284, 30337, 30718/29 before the end of the year. Unfortunately, by this date withdrawal had been recommenced in earnest and few members of the class were granted the expense of general overhaul and a repaint, only Nos 30120, 30313/38, 30701 in 1958 and No. 30707 in March 1959 being so favoured. Lined black remained the livery, which between 1949 and 1959 was carried by Nos 30117/20, 30282/3/4/5/7/8/9, 30300/1/2/4/7/10/3/36/7/8, 30702/3/15/6/7/8/9/21/4/5/6/7/8/9/30/2. In addition, of course, No 30119 ran painted malachite green. When this engine was being broken up at Ashford Works in February 1953, the opportunity was taken to scrape the paint from the cab sidesheets in an attempt to discover if any evidence of the pre-war olive green remained. It did, under two coats of malachite and one of black, but more interesting was the eventual emergence of London & South Western colours beneath several coats of Maunsell sage green.

The withdrawal of Nos 30284/5, 30337, 30705/12/21/7 took place in 1958, while Nos 30289, 30301/10, 30702/6/10/1/2/6/32 followed in 1959. At Nine Elms regular work on van services, empty stock duties and other mundane activities kept several of the class fully occupied until 17 June 1959, when the last two based there, Nos 30338 and 30719, departed for the West Country double heading an eight-coach troop train empty from Clapham Yard to Farnborough and loaded from there to Yeovil. Both afterwards made their way to Exmouth Junction. No 30732 remained at Guildford, although officially transferred to Eastleigh, and appeared daily on the Redhill–Reading services until late August 1959, when it was finally despatched to Eastleigh from where withdrawal took place in the autumn.

Despite a reduction in numbers and a lowering of status much life remained in the survivors, with No 30313 proving this on 19 August 1959, when the through 4.55pm Bristol–Portsmouth train was taken over late from a Western Region Hall at Salisbury. Notwithstanding the six heavily-laden coaches and a van, the nine miles to Dean were covered in 13min with a maximum speed of 72mph and Southampton Central was reached in 30¾min start to stop as against the 37 scheduled. The remainder of the journey was

Distance miles	*Location*	*Schedule min/sec*	*Actual min/sec*	*Speeds mph*
0.00	St Budeaux depart	0.00	0.00	
2.25	Tamerton Foliot		3.59	49½ (max)
4.10	Bere Ferrers		7.07	30
6.80	Bere Alston		13.26	24½
9.00	Milepost 218 summit		16.30	44½/36
13.30	Tavistock (arrive)	24.00	22.26	56 (max)
1.70	Milepost 212 summit		4.32	36
5.20	Brentor		10.03	47/30
6.50	Lydford		12.24	32½
9.70	Bridestowe		16.56	39/45
12.95	Milepost 200¾ summit		20.57	52/43
16.40	Okehampton (arrive)	28.00	25.28	60 (after braking)
3.60	Sampford Courtenay		5.45	60
6.50	North Tawton		8.08	77½
9.60	Bow		10.46	75
12.30	Milepost 185		13.00	78 (max)
14.40	Yeoford		15.36	45 (after braking)
18.10	Crediton (arrive)	25.00	20.20	60

Above: At work in the West Country, No 30711 heads the 10.02am Plymouth–Exeter–Waterloo, Atlantic Coast Express, out of Tavistock North in May 1959.
[S. C. Nash

equally enterprising with a right time arrival. Again, on 6 August 1960, No 30718 with the 2.33pm (SO) Plymouth–Exeter Central left 8½min late, but by Crediton had regained seven of these, and would have arrived to time but for the usual delays in and around Exeter St David's. The load was four coaches (131 tons) to Okehampton and seven (229 tons tare) thence to Exeter, while the weather varied from bright sunshine to heavy rain storms. Details are in the table. Features of the journey were the excellent acceleration, freedom from slip and abundance of steam.

In the West Country T9 workings varied little throughout the year, although on summer Saturdays there were a number of additional turns. One (SX) piloted the 5.10am Exeter to Okehampton and then worked the 7am Okehampton to Plymouth, returning on the 10.2am Plymouth to Okehampton. Other regular duties were the 9.56am Okehampton–Padstow, returning at 3.13pm to Exeter, the 1.18pm Okehampton–Bude, returning at 3.17pm, and the 5.51pm Okehampton–Padstow, which returned at 6pm from Padstow on the following day.

Eastleigh similarly found the class most useful and employed No 30120 on 5 March 1960 to work the last passenger train from Newbury to Eastleigh, while No 30707 had a regular job on the 10.57am Salisbury–Portsmouth vans. No 30729 on 18 September 1960 worked up to Waterloo with an enthusiasts' special from Salisbury and subsequently was employed by Nine Elms on the Reading vans before being

Below: The Greyhounds finally forsake the London area: Nos 30338 and 30718 are transfered to Exmouth Junction on 17 June 1959, working a Farnborough–Yeovil troop special.
[S. C. Nash

sent back to Exeter on a permanent way special later in the week.

By the winter of 1960/61, No 30707 was the only Greyhound working regularly east of Exeter, usually on the Portsmouth–Salisbury vans, but occasionally replacing Q class 0-6-0s on local goods turns. On 16 March 1961 it was laid aside on Eastleigh shed awaiting breaking up, its place shortly taken by No 30117, which was steamed on 25 March after some considerable time in store, and almost at once despatched to Nine Elms for an enthusiasts' special. It returned to Eastleigh with the 10.02am Herne Hill–Redbridge materials empties on 17 April, and after a boiler washout and inspection was set to work on the van services until 1 May. Use was then made of it on the Netley line fruit specials for some weeks in turn with BR class 4 2-6-0s before the end came on 24 June 1961, when the motion plate fractured at the head of the 5.05pm Botley–Southampton Central vans.

In the West Country Nos 30313, 30709/15/7 were joined in March 1961 by No 30120 from Eastleigh; en route it worked the Westward Television train, which at the period was touring Dorset, Wiltshire, Somerset and Devon. It subsequently took a share of the daily working to Plymouth which left Okehampton at 7am and return on the 10.02am Plymouth to Waterloo as far as Okehampton, this being a portion of the Atlantic Coast Express. On arrival at Okehampton the next duty was the 1.18pm to Bude and the 3.17pm return. By mid May only Nos 30120, 30313 and 30709 remained serviceable and available for these Okehampton cyclic turns, and two N class 2-6-0s had to be co-opted to fill the gaps. No 30313 was obviously the star performer, with consistently lively work up the North Cornwall banks, No 30120 was in reasonably good order, but No 30709 was visibly ailing. An additional duty often brought loads of 650 to 700 tons, this being the 5.10pm (SX) quarry workers train from Meldon to Okehampton, which in addition to a passenger coach often included a full load of ballast hoppers for despatch from Okehampton later in the evening. As the two-mile run was entirely downhill at 1 in 77, the driver was more worried by the problem of stopping than stalling. During the last week of June 1961 the axe finally fell and all five engines were despatched to Eastleigh for withdrawal, Nos 30120 and 30313 on a ballast special to Salisbury and No 30709 towing Nos 30715/7. The other remaining Greyhound, No. 30287, had been rusting away in store from the autumn of 1959 and was unlikely to work again so the Drummond 4-4-0s had at long last come to the end of their days. The Southern Region was the poorer by their going.

For some years the preservation of a rebuilt Greyhound had been under consideration and now a final decision had to be made. At first the oldest remaining survivor, No 30117, was chosen, but on inspection it was found beyond economic repair and was passed over in favour of No 30288. Later it, too, lost favour, with the final choice falling on the second oldest survivor, No 30120. Actual preservation commenced at Eastleigh Works towards the end of 1961 and was completed on 10 March 1962. Very wisely no attempt was made to return it to the pre-superheated state. Being rebuilt in May 1927, No 120 never carried South Western colours in its modernised guise, therefore Southern Railway livery would have been most appropriate, especially as the sandboxes had not been returned to the leading splashers. It was, however, painted South Western green and over the next year or so was employed by Eastleigh shed on various local passenger duties as well as for a number of enthusiasts' specials, including that to the Bluebell Railway on 15 September 1963, when it joined forces with, of all types, preserved Caledonian 4-2-2 No 123. The two Drummonds, one green and the other blue, made a fine sight. After a period of store at Fratton, it was despatched to Stratford (ER) in September 1964 and to Preston Park, Brighton, Pullman Car Shops in February 1968 before being transferred to Tyseley for reconditioning in September 1970.

Above: Two Drummond engines pass Purley on 15 September 1963 with the Bluebell Special, preserved Caledonian single, blue No 123, piloting LSW green T9, No 120. *[S. C. Nash*

Below: Preserved and restored T9 4-4-0 No 120 stands at Eastleigh shed in May 1963. *[E. W. Fry*

CHAPTER ELEVEN

ACCIDENTS AND OTHER KINDRED MISHAPS

Because of human error or structural failure all railways on occasion suffer accidents and the London & South Western was no exception. Therefore, with a class of locomotives as numerous, hard working and long lasting as the Greyhounds it was inevitable that over the years a number would become involved in accidents and other mishaps. Fortunately, with the notable exception of Salisbury in 1906, the South Western, by a combination of good management and luck, was able to avoid those catastrophic happenings which seemed to afflict the northern lines. Admittedly, the company operated few heavy main line loose-coupled goods trains, always a prime source of trouble, but the density of traffic around London was probably the highest in the country. Credit must also be granted to engine crews, guards, signalmen and other officials for consistently displaying such a high standard of self-discipline and attention to the company's rules and regulations.

The Greyhounds delivered by Dübs & Co in 1899/1900 completed their thousand-mile trial periods without mishap, but shortly afterwards No 712 failed with a broken driving axle when running into Woking with a Salisbury semi-fast. No injuries occurred, but damage to the motion, cylinders and ashpan was severe. A few days later on 8 March 1900, a similar mishap befell No 704 between Hinton Admiral and Christchurch, while No 726 on 12 March 1900 was laid aside at Salisbury with suspected movement between its driving wheels and axle. Drummond at once ordered an inspection of all axles when those of Nos 703/10/31 were found defective. Dübs accepted responsibility and provided replacements at a cost of £94.68, including labour at Nine Elms Works.

Some initial trouble was also met with the regulators which, when suddenly opened after a period of closure, stubbornly refused to shut. This undesirable property led No 117 into difficulties at Bournemouth West on 19 December 1899 when backing down on to a Waterloo express. It hit the coaches at about 10mph causing severe damage to its tender as well as to the front half of the train and a lengthy section of platform edging. Only the engine crew, a guard and a shunter were slightly injured, the train being empty. A similar minor incident occurred to No 709 at Exmouth Junction shed on 29 December 1899 when it crashed into T1 class 0-4-4 tank No 364 near the coaling stage. The regulators of all engines were thereupon inspected and many found faulty because of the maker's misinterpretation of the drawings and failure to allow sufficient clearance for expansion.

Bournemouth West on 19 September 1903 was again the scene of an accident when No 709 and Adams 4-4-0 No 662 were despatched together from the depot at the Central station to run there to collect their trains for Waterloo and Salisbury respectively. At Gas Works Junction No 709's firemen walked along the running plate to uncouple the Adams while moving at about 5mph and then signalled to his driver to proceed towards the coaches of the 7.50am Waterloo express. As they were approached Driver Robey ordered an application of the handbrake and, when this proved inadequate, applied the vacuum brake before reversing the engine and giving a prolonged warning blast on his whistle. There was no apparent reduction in speed and at about 15mph No 709, running tender first, majestically ploughed into the train while the crew, and a guard travelling on the footplate, frantically baled out on to the platform. Damage was severe with the first three vehicles, Pullman car *Princess Margaret*, third bogie brake No 114 and second/third bogie compo No 581 being telescoped into each other and the remaining seven coaches partially derailed and crushed against the platform coping. For a few moments all was quiet, then with a snort and slipping of wheels No 709, under fully open regulator and in fore-gear, began leaving the station and setting off in the general direction of Poole with no-one on the footplate. Fortunately, a goods guard realised the danger and by sprinting across the tracks was able to board the runaway and shut off the steam. Apart from the crew no-one was injured, for the station foreman was quick to appreciate the situation and possessing a strident voice warned the intending passengers to keep clear. At the subsequent inquiry Driver Robey was blamed for the occurrence, having been found guilty on three counts: not stopping to uncouple engines at Gas Works Junction

Dugald Drummond's Car, known to the men as 'The Bug'.

signalbox, failing to connect the brake hoses of the two engines, and approaching the train at reckless speed. Drummond immediately dismissed Driver Robey and his fireman, suspended the guard travelling on the footplate for seven days and asked the directors to award the guard who stopped No 709 with three days' holiday and £10.

The next incident occurred on 8 March 1904, when No 284 was standing at signals near Clapham Junction and was struck violently by a London & North Western 0-6-0 which had come across London with a train of horse boxes destined for the army at Pirbright. Some confusion with signals had caused the foreign crew to imagine that the way was clear into Clapham Yards when in fact they should have stopped several hundred yards back. Speed was low and, apart from some crushing of No 284's tender, damage was minor, although a shunter was flung violently on to the track and required hospital treatment. The same engine was again in trouble on 30 October 1904 when it crashed into a platelayer's trolley near Tisbury station and derailed its bogie. The rest of the train remained on the track and damage was restricted to broken carriage windows and track chairs.

Bournemouth was once more the scene of an affray affecting the class when on 24 April 1904 No 702 worked down from Waterloo with the 7.55am express and retired to the shed for turning and coaling. This accomplished, it was moved into a short bay on the up side of the Central station to await the road for Bournemouth West. However, before this was available, dock tank No 103 and seven loaded coal wagons ran out of control down the bank from the shed and thrust 702 bodily into the gents toilet, much to the horror and embarrassment of the occupants who hurriedly escaped to the platform, unharmed except for their dignity. The smokebox and front framing of No 702 was extensively damaged, while the tender was not considered worth repairing and was scrapped.

Drummond was not only head of the Locomotive Department but also in charge of the Running Department and the engine sheds. In these various capacities he felt duty-bound to roam far and wide about the system to ensure personally that his instructions and the company's business was being strictly adhered to at all times. This proved no mean task and led to excessive time being spent away from headquarters. To reduce these absences to acceptable levels and gain greater freedom of movement, the Locomotive Committee in August 1898 alloted £1,765 for the construction of a compact single-driver locomotive with a small saloon positioned to the rear of the cab. It entered service in June 1899 and was officially known as *Mr Drummond's Car*, although the men invariably preferred the more apt, if less dignified, title of *The Bug*. Over the next decade this Machiavellian oddity became a familiar sight all over the South Western and, with its swift and often unscheduled appearance at places far distant from the seat of authority, was the cause of much foreboding in the hearts of those not abiding strictly to the rule book. The express passenger head code was exhibited at all times and Drummond insisted on having privileged treatment from signalmen en route.

It was while so engaged on 10 June 1908 that Drummond passed No 708 near Sutton Bingham running about 13min late with an up West of England express. Drummond was fully aware of its tardiness and was leaning out of the saloon window looking for the delinquent and attempting to discover the cause of delay. Eventually seeing No 708 approaching in some distress he was horrified to observe the smokebox door swing open to give him a glimpse of some two hundred grinning tubes. He was not impressed and at once had *The Bug* brought to a halt by the Sutton Bingham signalbox and with no delay had it crossed over to the up line before setting off at speed towards Yeovil Junction where, as expected, No 708 was in the process of being replaced. The Black Book fails to report Drummond's words on arrival, but his actions are quite clear. No 708 went back post haste on to the train and, with the smokebox door secured, departed for Waterloo with Drummond and the fireman of *The Bug* in charge of the footplate. At the subsequent discussion of the subject Driver Howard was fined £6 and reduced to shunting duties while Fireman Best received a £4 fine and a severe warning.

Many other stories have been told of Drummond's exploits and travels in his *Car*, but only one other relates to the Greyhounds. This took place at Salisbury on 23 May 1911 when No 113 was being moved from the coaling stage to the turntable by a passed fireman named Nicholls. As the movement commenced the *Car* came to rest in the yards and Drummond clambered down to view the scene in his usual jaundiced manner. The unfortunate Nicholls was so impressed by the sight at close range that he completely forgot to note the table's position and at a walking pace approached the pit tender first. Noticing this, Drummond at once roared a warning and waved both arms, but all to no avail for Nicholls became petrified with fear and No 113 slowly and surely trundled into the turntable pit. It was reasonably quickly retrieved and effects on other traffic were minimal, but nevertheless Nicholls was fined £3 and demoted to fireman.

At this period the South Western only possessed five breakdown cranes with a combined lifting capacity of 75 tons, therefore the majority of re-railing activities involved the use of jacks, packing and the haulage power of other locomotives. Unless a derailment was particularly bad most depots managed operations with their own resources. The five cranes were located as follows:

Location	*Number*	*Maximum lift tons*	*Radius ft*	*Remarks*
Nine Elms	1	20	21	Self-propelled
Guildford	2	10	18	Self-propelled
Salisbury	3	15	19	
Eastleigh	4	10	18	Self-propelled
Exmouth Junction	5	20	21	Self-propelled

Of more consequence was the collision at Vauxhall station on 29 August 1912, when No 312 was running light engine from Nine Elms shed to Waterloo before taking away the 8.30am Union boat express to Southampton Docks. The 6.37am Aldershot–Waterloo semi-fast hauled by M7 No 247 had just stopped at the up through platform at Vauxhall when it was run into from the rear by No 312 at about 15mph. The impact was severe, with the last two coaches being demolished and the remaining six variously battered, while No 312's tender had its frames fractured, the tank ripped open and much of the side plating torn off. By good fortune only one passenger was travelling in the rear first class coach; he was killed instantly while 50 more in the next two coaches were injured, many seriously. At the subsequent inquiry the driver of the light engine was found guilty of misreading the signals and accepting those for the up main local line whereas in reality he was running on the up through line.

The next accident, on 17 February 1913, commenced on quite a minor key, but eventually cost the company no less than £14,000 before all claims had been settled. At 11.05am No 118 was approaching Woking with a Poole–Waterloo excursion when the piston head broke, wrecking the right-hand cylinder and causing the train to stop about a quarter mile on the Basingstoke side of the platforms. Prompt action was taken to notify the signalbox and protect the rear of the train, but the guard and crew forgot to inspect the other tracks and when 700 class No 694 passed at reduced speed it was derailed by debris from No 118. No-one was injured, but a prize bull was killed and a valuable consignment of Persian carpets were damaged by colza oil seeping from a tanker wagon. The driver of No 118 was found to blame and, considering the consequences, escaped very lightly when given a £3 fine and three days' suspension from duty.

Wagons left on the running lines during shunting operations and then forgotten were the cause of several accidents during the war years, although only one directly concerned the class, occurring on 7 August 1915, when No 310 at the head of the nine-coach 8.50am Waterloo–Exeter express was approaching Wilton at 55mph. The driver observed the wagons at a distance of 480yd, and at once applied the brakes, sanded the rails and reversed his engine, but was unable to stop and hit the obstruction at about 20mph. The three wagons were completely demolished, 335yd of permanent way distorted and 50 chairs smashed, but by good fortune No 310 and its train remained on the track. There were five injuries, three being soldiers in the front coach who, on realising an accident was imminent, had jumped off the train before the point of impact. One wedged his foot so tightly in a small culvert that his removal for medical attention was delayed until a section of piping was broken off and despatched with him to hospital. At the inquiry the driver of the morning pick-up goods admitted responsibility, although a fractured coupling hook was the real culprit. As the goods train moved off into the down yards there was some snatching of the couplings and one previously flawed proved unable to take the sudden stress and parted, leaving the last three wagons in the path of the express. The driver or guard should have noticed the occurrence, but in their haste to prepare for departure at 12.20pm immediately after the express, they failed to note the line was obstructed. Only three windows and some buffing gear were broken on the train, but No 312 suffered a buckled buffer beam, fractured buffers, stove in smokebox, broken blast and steam pipes and the loss of some boiler sheeting. The left-hand clack box was ripped off and this led to firebox damage before the fire could be thrown out. The total cost of repairs to No 312, the train and the permanent way was £983.

From the earliest days of rail travel fog formed a source of worry, frustration, and danger because of its interference with visibility and was the direct cause of numerous collisions and other mishaps despite the strict application of safety rules. Some were serious, but fortunately most were minor affrays quickly forgotten. One such occurred at 7pm on 3 February 1921 at Queen's Road station when M7 class 0-4-4 tank No 374 crashed at about 10mph into the rear of the 10-coach 5.54pm Waterloo–Woking headed by No 283. Forty-seven passengers were injured, but none killed because the rear coach had been filled with mailbags destined for Guildford after the train normally conveying them had been cancelled.

The last South Western accident – indeed only 11min before the LSWR ceased to exist – happened at 11.49pm on 31 December 1922, when No 116 was passing Eastleigh station on the through road with a White Star boat special for Southampton Docks. Suddenly the coupling between the engine and tender parted, leaving the former, with the crew huddled precariously on the footplate, being hotly pursued by its tender and the nine-coach train. The driver wisely decided to increase speed and keep clear until breakage of the vacuum system caused a brake application and brought both train and tender to a halt.

Under Southern Railway ownership there were a number of minor accidents and one involving 27 casualties at Woking on 10 November 1945. Probably the most unusual incident occurred on 26 February 1925, when on a foggy morning No 718 was working empty stock from the sidings at Eastleigh to Winchester where it was to form a troop special. After coupling on the train at Eastleigh the shunter unwisely walked round the front of the engine as it was starting away and by mischance tripped over the rails and fell against the buffer beam. His stout leather belt engaged with the coupling hook leaving him suspended above the track as the train gathered speed. He shouted for help but to no avail until the Winchester stop where he was released and despatched to hospital. Apart from some bruising of the ribs, strained stomach muscles and loss of voice he was found unscathed by the ordeal.

Of a similar minor nature was the meeting head-on between Alton and Medstead & Four Marks of No 114 and a large cock pheasant. The latter was feeding on the track side as the train approached when for no apparent reason it flew straight at the engine, glanced off the dome cover and dived through the left-hand lookout window. The driver was cut by flying glass, but was able to take the train on to Eastleigh where he was relieved for hospital treatment, and departed with the offending bird firmly installed in his overcoat pocket. It was quite common for smaller birds to be killed by trains, although rare for pheasants to be hit.

Much more serious was the accident at Woking on Saturday, 10 November 1945, when No 119 was in charge of the eight-coach 4.54pm Waterloo–Basingstoke semi-fast and had been detained for several minutes by the through home signal. Just as it was getting under way and moving at about 8mph the rear coach was violently struck and telescoped for half its length by King Arthur No 452 *Sir Meliagrance* heading the 5pm Waterloo–Exeter express. No 119 was not badly damaged, but the King Arthur broke away from its train and came to rest about 400yd from the point of impact. Twenty-two passengers, the guard of the Basingstoke train and both engine crews suffered injury. At the subsequent inquiry it was found that the smoke beating down across the King Arthur's cab had caused the driver to misinterpret the signals to the extent that he was travelling at fully 60mph when the rear light of No 119's train was sighted. The Southern Railway was fortunate indeed to escape so lightly, although, of course, the Greyhounds had always been a lucky class.

APPENDICES

1 T9 CLASS HISTORIES

	BUILT			*SUPERHEATED*		
Engine No	*Date*	*Works*	*Makers or Order Nos*	*Date*	*British Railways No*	*Withdrawn*
113	June 1899	Nine Elms	G9	November 1925	—	May 1951
114	June 1899	Nine Elms	G9	November 1927	—	May 1951
115	July 1899	Nine Elms	G9	August 1927	30115	May 1951
116	July 1899	Nine Elms	G9	August 1925	—	April 1951
117	July 1899	Nine Elms	G9	November 1927	30117	July 1961
118	July 1899	Nine Elms	G9	June 1928	—	May 1951
119	August 1899	Nine Elms	G9	October 1923	30119	December 1952
120	August 1899	Nine Elms	G9	May 1927	30120	July 1963
121	September 1899	Nine Elms	G9	February 1924	30121	April 1951
122	September 1899	Nine Elms	G9	April 1926	30122	March 1951
280	October 1899	Nine Elms	K9	July 1927	—	May 1951
281	November 1899	Nine Elms	K9	June 1928	30281	October 1951
282	November 1899	Nine Elms	K9	December 1923	30282	March 1954
283	November 1899	Nine Elms	K9	October 1925	30283	December 1957
284	November 1899	Nine Elms	K9	July 1923	30284	April 1958
285	January 1900	Nine Elms	O9	January 1926	30285	June 1958
286	February 1900	Nine Elms	O9	June 1926	30286	April 1951
287	February 1900	Nine Elms	O9	January 1924	30287	August 1961
288	February 1900	Nine Elms	O9	February 1926	30288	December 1960
289	February 1900	Nine Elms	O9	December 1927	30289	November 1959
300	December 1900	Nine Elms	T9	October 1922	30300	March 1961
301	December 1900	Nine Elms	T9	January 1923	30301	August 1959
302	December 1900	Nine Elms	T9	June 1923	30302	September 1952
303	January 1901	Nine Elms	T9	April 1923	—	May 1951
304	January 1901	Nine Elms	T9	June 1922	30304	September 1957
305	February 1901	Nine Elms	X9	July 1922	—	April 1951
307	February 1901	Nine Elms	X9	August 1924	30307	December 1952
310	April 1901	Nine Elms	X9	March 1923	30310	May 1959
311	April 1901	Nine Elms	X9	December 1922	30311	July 1952
312	May 1901	Nine Elms	X9	February 1925	30312	January 1952
313	May 1901	Nine Elms	G10	July 1922	30313	July 1961
314	May 1901	Nine Elms	G10	April 1922	—	May 1951
336	September 1901	Nine Elms	G10	March 1923	30336	February 1953
337	September 1901	Nine Elms	G10	May 1925	30337	December 1958
338	October 1901	Nine Elms	G10	January 1923	30338	April 1961
702	February 1899	Dübs & Co	3746	May 1923	30702	October 1959
703	February 1899	Dübs & Co	3747	September 1926	30703	September 1952
704	February 1899	Dübs & Co	3748	June 1923	30704	October 1951
705	February 1899	Dübs & Co	3749	May 1924	30705	January 1958
706	February 1899	Dübs & Co	3750	September 1925	30706	May 1959
707	June 1899	Dübs & Co	3751	October 1924	30707	March 1961
708	June 1899	Dübs & Co	3752	May 1927	30708	December 1957
709	June 1899	Dübs & Co	3753	June 1923	30709	July 1961
710	June 1899	Dübs & Co	3754	July 1929	30710	March 1959
711	June 1899	Dübs & Co	3755	August 1927	30711	August 1959
712	June 1899	Dübs & Co	3756	March 1928	30712	November 1958
713	June 1899	Dübs & Co	3757	July 1925	—	April 1951
714	July 1899	Dübs & Co	3758	February 1924	30714	March 1951
715	July 1899	Dübs & Co	3759	December 1923	30715	July 1961
716	September 1899	Dübs & Co	3760	July 1927	30716	October 1951
717	September 1899	Dübs & Co	3761	September 1927	30717	July 1961
718	September 1899	Dübs & Co	3762	September 1928	30718	March 1961
719	September 1899	Dübs & Co	3763	August 1926	30719	March 1961
721	September 1899	Dübs & Co	3764	August 1923	30721	July 1958
722	September 1899	Dübs & Co	3765	October 1923	—	April 1951
723	September 1899	Dübs & Co	3766	May 1928	—	June 1951
724	October 1899	Dübs & Co	3767	May 1923	30724	May 1959
725	October 1899	Dübs & Co	3768	February 1926	30725	December 1952
726	October 1899	Dübs & Co	3769	February 1924	30726	August 1959
727	October 1899	Dübs & Co	3770	May 1925	30727	September 1958
728	January 1900	Dübs & Co	3771	January 1926	30728	September 1956
729	January 1900	Dübs & Co	3772	August 1923	30729	March 1961
730	January 1900	Dübs & Co	3773	December 1927	30730	August 1957
731	January 1900	Dübs & Co	3774	January 1927	—	May 1951
732	January 1900	Dübs & Co	3775	March 1927	30732	October 1959
773	December 1901	Dübs & Co	4038	June 1923	30733	April 1952

Renumberings: 773 became 733 in December 1924.
Final mileages: No 117 – 1,982,396; No 119 – 1,543,560; No 120 – 1,713,304; No 280 – 1,411,617; No 287 – 1,927,593; No 301 – 1,819,562; No 338 – 1,879,273; No 711 – 1,896,489; No 714 – 1,746,960; No 717 – 2,064,689; No 729 – 2,001,226; No 773 (733) – 1,477,899.
Oil burners: Nos 113/4/5/8/21, 280/6, 303/5/14, 713/22/31.
Preservation: No 120 in LSWR livery is preserved by the Birmingham Railway Museum, Tyseley, but at the time of writing was not in working order. Most of the class were broken up at the rear of Eastleigh Works, but Brighton Works dealt with Nos 30304, 30712, and Ashford Works with Nos 30119, 30282, 30301/2/7/11/2, 30702/3/11/25/6/33. The tender tops and water tanks from 16 engines were salvaged and fitted to the frames and wheels of tenders belonging to ex LB&SCR C2X class 0-6-0 goods. The result was reasonably aesthetic and not as unsightly as was to be expected from the marrying together of such a queer mixture of tender parts.

2 THE URIE POWER CLASSIFICATION

In March 1916 Robert Urie introduced a lettered power classification for all main line locomotives, with 'A' representing the highest power. These letters were painted on the platform valance immediately behind the buffer beams, or on the older Adams and Beyer Peacock goods on the sandboxes or the splashers. At the time of introduction it was stated that the classification was not based on tractive effort alone, but also upon the boiler and braking power. Superheating, except in the case of F13 class 4-6-0 No 333 was not taken into account and locomotives of the same class using saturated or superheated steam were allotted the same letter. The full list printed in the working timetables is shown in the table, right.

After Grouping, the Southern Railway retained this classification for Western Section locomotives, and applied it to Lord Nelson, King Arthur, Schools and Q classes, the first three becoming 'A' and the last 'B'. It remained in use until the introduction of the British Railways power classification when for a time some locomotives carried both systems on the cabsides.

Letter	*Classes*
A	H15, N15, S15, H16, G16, F13 (No 333)
B	G14, P14, T14, F13 (Nos 330/1/2/4 relegated from 'A')
C	700
D	D15, L12
E	S11
F	K10, L11
G	0395
H	T9 (Greyhounds)
I	C8, E10, T3, T6, T7, X2, X6
J	A12, 0380, double-framed 0-6-0s
K	M7, T1, 0135, 0445, 0460, 046, 0415, single-framed 0-6-0s (relegated from 'J')
Not classified	B4, C14, F9 (*The Bug*), G6, O2, Beattie well tanks, 0330, Terrier No 735, 0-4-0 tanks, Nos 734, 0111, 0408, 0458

BIBLIOGRAPHY

North British Railway Minute books 1875–83
North British Railway Directors' Report and Accounts 1875–83
Caledonian Railway:
- Minute books of Directors and Committees 1882–92
- Working timetables
- Locomotive Department's file of extracts from Minutes of Board Meetings and relative letters 1882–92
  - St Rollox boiler-proving register
- Locomotive register
- Specification for 4-4-0 No 124 by Dübs & Co.

London & South Western Railway:
- Minute books of Directors and Locomotive Committee 1895–1922
- Locomotive Registers 1895–1923
- Boiler, Firebox and Cylinder Registers 1895–1923
- Tender Register 1901–23
- Mileage Register 1895–1923
- Trials Register
- Coaching Stock Registers 1895–1923
- Working timetables 1899–1913
- Accident reports 1899–1922

Dugald Drummond's personal diaries
Southern Railway:
- Eastleigh, Ashford and Brighton Works repair registers
- Engine record cards
- Boiler record book and cards
- Mileage records
- Locomotive diagram books
- Eastleigh locomotive drawings

The Railway Observer and Stephenson Locomotive Society Journal 1930 to 1961
Various copies of the Railway Magazine
London & South Western Railway Magazine

INDEX